ESSENTIAL
ACADEMIC
VOCABULARY

Mastering the Complete Academic Word List

HELEN HUNTLEY
West Virginia University

Australia • Brazil • Japan • Korea • Mexico • Singapore • Spain • United Kingdom • United States

Essential Academic Vocabulary:
Mastering the Complete Academic Word List
Helen Huntley

Publisher: Patricia A. Coryell

Director of ESL Publishing: Susan Maguire

Senior Development Editor: Kathy Sands Boehmer

Editorial Assistant: Evangeline Bermas

Project Editor: Kerry Doyle

Senior Marketing Manager: Annamarie Rice

Marketing Assistant: Andrew Whitacre

Cover Image: Eric Bean/Getty Images

Text credits are on page xi.

Library of Congress Control Number: 2005925065

ISBN-13: 978-0-618-44542-4

ISBN-10: 0-618-44542-0

National Geographic Learning
20 Channel Center Street
Boston, MA 02210
USA

Cengage Learning is a leading provider of customized learning solutions with office locations around the globe, including Singapore, the United Kingdom, Australia, Mexico, Brazil, and Japan. Locate your local office at **www.cengage.com/global**

Cengage Learning products are represented in Canada by Nelson Education, Ltd.

Visit National Geographic Learning at **elt.heinle.com**

Visit our corporate website at **www.cengage.com**

Printed in the United States of America
14 15 16 17 18   20 19 18 17 16

CONTENTS

Welcome to
Essential Academic Vocabulary

To The Instructor

Essential Academic Vocabulary addresses the needs of native speakers of English and English as a Second Language (ESL) students in college preparatory, community college, and university programs who must acquire the type of vocabulary commonly used in college undergraduate and graduate programs in all disciplines. In addition, much of this vocabulary is useful in all sections of the Test of English as a Foreign Language (TOEFL), which for most international students is the hurdle that must be crossed for college admission in the United States. The text can be used by students studying in the United States, as well as by students taking English courses in other countries. The text is designed for one fifteen- or sixteen-week semester or for two sequential quarters; it could also be adapted for other courses of different lengths.

The Academic Word List

Essential Academic Vocabulary is based on the Academic Word List (AWL), which was developed in 2000 by Averil Coxhead at Victoria University in Wellington, New Zealand. The list was developed from a written academic corpus for use by higher-education students in the fields of liberal arts, commerce, law, and science. The AWL contains 570 headwords of word families, divided into ten sublists according to range and frequency. It excludes the first 2,000 words of English from the General Service List (developed in 1953), technical and specialist terms, proper nouns, and Latin forms.

The targeted vocabulary words in each chapter appear in a tabular format and then are introduced through an academic reading text that has been minimally adapted. The reading texts have been chosen from current introductory-level college textbooks in many of the academic disciplines from which the AWL was originally compiled. The targeted words are sequenced more or less according to the frequency accorded them in the AWL. However, the necessity of fitting words into authentic academic texts required some deviation from this sequence.

The AWL was divided into sixteen chapters to correspond to the number of weeks in a typical semester, with an additional review chapter after every four chapters. All chapters include extensive review, and communicative activities for reading, writing, and speaking have been developed to practice the targeted vocabulary words in a specific academic context. In addition, the level of complexity of the reading texts and associated practice activities increases as the level of difficulty of the vocabulary words rises.

Focus on Memory Research

The activities in the textbook are based on the "Eleven Principles for Learning Vocabulary," described by N. Schmitt and D. Schmitt in *Eleven Principles for Designing a Vocabulary Curriculum* ("Vocabulary Notebooks: Theoretical Underpinnings and Practical Suggestions," *English Language Teaching Journal,* 1995), as follows:

- The best way to remember new words is to incorporate them into language that is already known.
- Organized material is easier to learn.

- Words that are very similar should not be learned at the same time.

- Word pairs (native word/English word) can be used to learn many words in a short time.

- Knowing a word entails more than just knowing its meaning.

- The deeper the mental processing used when learning a word, the more likely that a learner will remember it.

- The act of recalling a word makes it more likely that a learner will recall it again later.

- Learners must pay close attention to learn most effectively.

- Words need to be recycled to be learned.

- An efficient recycling method involves expanding rehearsal.

- Learners are individuals and have different learning styles.

Text Organization

Each chapter follows a similar format designed to preview, learn, and practice the vocabulary words in a real academic context:

- **Illustration:** A photograph or an illustration introduces the chapter theme.

- **Word List:** Thirty to forty vocabulary words are introduced in each chapter. They are presented in a tabular format and organized according to the parts of speech: nouns, verbs, adjectives, adverbs, and other parts of speech. Word meanings are not provided. Students are expected to prepare for class by consulting an English-English dictionary (a monolingual English dictionary for ESL learners) and by writing unknown words on vocabulary cards or in a vocabulary notebook.

- **Preview Questions:** Discussion questions activate the students' background knowledge.

- **Reading:** A reading adapted from an up-to-date undergraduate textbook highlights the chapter vocabulary. The reading topics have been chosen to interest a wide variety of students but do not require any prerequisite technical knowledge.

- **Vocabulary in Context:** Students are required to choose the best meaning of a word according to the context in which the vocabulary word is used in the reading.

- **Reading Comprehension (Text Analysis):** Students complete a variety of exercises, including making inferences, completing charts, and answering questions designed to assess comprehension of the text and the vocabulary.

- **Dictionary Skills:** A dictionary entry for one vocabulary item from the chapter list is highlighted for study. Students complete a variety of exercises that require them to understand and use the information in the dictionary.

- **Word Forms:** Students complete charts with different word forms of vocabulary words from the chapter. Then students use these word forms to complete sentences or paragraphs.

- **Collocations:** Collocational phrases and verb/adjective/noun combinations are introduced. Students use this information to create original sentences or to identify meanings.

- **Word Parts:** Each chapter introduces a Latin or Greek prefix or base or several suffixes that relate to a word in the chapter vocabulary list. This is followed by practice in identifying the meanings of other words that incorporate the same features.

- **Writing (Task-Based Activity and Paragraph Writing):** The writing section consists of two parts. In a task-based activity, students perform an academic writing task, such as paraphrasing, summarizing, writing a definition, or writing a lab report. In paragraph writing, students are encouraged to use their own experiences or opinions to reflect on one of two topics introduced in the chapter.

- **Speaking (Partner or Group Activity and Role-Plays):** The speaking section also consists of two parts. In the partner or group activity, students participate in an academic speaking task, such as giving a presentation, conducting a survey, interviewing, explaining a chart, or summarizing a reading passage orally. In the role-plays, students engage in spontaneous interactions chosen from two topics introduced in the chapter.

Appendices

The text includes the following appendices:

- Getting the Most from Your Dictionary (with practice exercises)

- Suggestions for Learning and Reviewing Vocabulary

- Techniques for Paraphrasing

- Techniques for Summarizing

- Word Parts and Their Meanings: A complete alphabetical listing with chapter references for word parts that were presented in the text

- The Academic Word List: An alphabetical listing of words with the corresponding chapter of introduction

Websites

The text is reinforced by companion websites with links for teachers and students. The instructor website contains the answer key, textbook and chapter notes, course schedules, sample syllabus, and downloadable quizzes. The student website provides a complete chapter listing of vocabulary, additional Internet resources for learning vocabulary, and online review exercises. For these, go to **elt.heinle.com/essentialvocab**

TO THE STUDENT

Essential Academic Vocabulary is designed to answer your needs as a student preparing to start academic coursework or preparing for the TOEFL. Understandably, you may be worried that you may have difficulty with the TOEFL reading section or with the large amount of required reading in your academic courses because of your limited vocabulary knowledge. However, this textbook should help you learn and practice the words you need to know and increase your self-confidence.

The textbook is based on the Academic Word List, which consists of 570 words commonly used in most academic fields. Whether you are going to study physics, art, or linguistics, knowledge of these words will help you understand your lectures, read academic textbooks, and write term papers. The textbook contains many more than 570 words, however. You will learn all forms and meanings of the words (noun, verb, adjective, adverb), useful phrases that contain these words, and roots and prefixes that can be added to make new words. The words are introduced to you in academic readings on topics ranging from business to geology to information technology and are practiced in a variety of academic writing and speaking activities related to the topic.

After studying and practicing the words in this textbook, you should be able to read an academic text with knowledge of about 95 percent of the words. This accomplishment will make your effort in learning the words truly worthwhile. Your own positive attitude and motivation toward vocabulary learning is very important for successful study. Your instructor and the textbook will help guide you toward your personal goals in enlarging your academic vocabulary, but it is important to remember that you are ultimately responsible for learning, practicing, and regularly reviewing these vocabulary words to achieve a successful outcome.

ACKNOWLEDGMENTS

The ideas and material for this book were developed over several years of teaching vocabulary courses to advanced students in the Intensive English Program at West Virginia University. I am indebted to my students for their reactions to the material, through which I gained the insights I needed to delete, adapt, and supplement where necessary. I would also like to thank Michael Wilhelm and Christy Limbaugh for piloting the textbook in their courses and providing me with feedback from a teacher's point of view. The writing of this book was encouraged and supported throughout its development by the dedicated team in the ESL College Division of Houghton Mifflin. In particular, I was inspired by the enthusiastic energy of Susan Maguire, ESL Director, and Joann Rishel Kozyrev, a former colleague and now a prolific textbook writer and ESL sales specialist for Houghton Mifflin. Many other people have encouraged me along the way and provided me with timely assistance: Kathy Sands Boehmer, Evangeline Bermas, and Annamarie Rice. Special thanks are due to my developmental editor, Angela Castro, who provided invaluable advice and feedback in the final stages of the book. Words of thanks also go to the following reviewers who provided helpful suggestions and ideas that shaped the revisions:

Donna Frankel, Bunker Hill Community College; Elisa Fazio, University of Louisville; Glenda Bro, Mt. San Antonio College; Jim Epstein, University of Arizona; Kate Dingle, Northeastern University; Maggie Discont, West Hills College; Mary Lu Light, Western Michigan University; Meredith Massey, Prince George's Community College; Michelle Schweitzer, Bunker Hill Community College; Miguel Lopez, College of the Desert; Shannon Bailey, Austin Community College

A final word of appreciation goes to my husband, David, and son, Simon, for their patience and support during this project.

TEXT CREDITS

Chapter 1: page 1: © Mike Richards/PhotoEdit; **page 2:** Reading, "Cooperative Learning," adapted from: "Key Elements of Successful Cooperative Learning," California Department of Education, accessed at http://www.cde.ca.gov/sp/el/er/cooplrng.asp, May 17, 2005; and *Student Cultural Diversity: Understanding and Meeting the Challenge,* 3rd ed., by Eugene Garcia (Houghton Mifflin Company, 2002, pp. 344–345).

Chapter 2: page 12: © Gary Conner/PhotoEdit; **page 13:** Reading, "Test Anxiety," adapted from *Connections: Orientation 1,* 2nd ed., by T. Anne Hawkins (West Virginia University, 2000, pp. 169, 176–177).

Chapter 3: page 22: © Myrleen Ferguson Cate/PhotoEdit.

Chapter 4: page 33: © Tony Freeman/PhotoEdit; **page 34:** Reading, "Extracurricular Activities: A Means to an End," adapted from *Extracurricular Options for Pre-meds,* Columbia College Web site (http://www.studentaffairs.columbia.edu/preprofessional/health/extra_curricular.php), accessed May 17, 2005.

Chapter 5: page 47: © Michael Newman/PhotoEdit.

Chapter 6: page 53: © Bill Aron/PhotoEdit; **page 54:** Reading, "Shifting Challenges in Education," adapted from *Student Cultural Diversity: Understanding and Meeting the Challenge,* 3rd ed., by Eugene Garcia (Houghton Mifflin Company, 2002, pp. 4–5).

Chapter 7: page 66: © David Young-Wolff/PhotoEdit; **page 67:** Reading, "Proctor & Gamble: An Optimistic Scheme," adapted from *Business,* 7th ed., by William M. Pride, Robert J. Hughes, and Jack R. Kapoor (Houghton Mifflin Company, 2002, p. 130); **page 76:** Paragraph Writing: Principles, from Proctor & Gamble (http://www.pg.com; 11/15/03).

Chapter 8: page 78: © David Simson/Stock Boston; **page 79:** Reading, "Marketing Tobacco Products around the World," adapted from *Business,* 7th ed., by William M. Pride, Robert J. Hughes, and Jack R. Kapoor (Houghton Mifflin Company, 2002, p. 361); **page 84:** Word Forms, "Tobacco Companies Target Traditional Women," adapted from Join Together Online, August 28, 2003 (http://www.jointogether.org/sa/news/summaries/reader/0,1854,566401,00.html8/2; 6/2003); **page 88:** Writing: Defining a Term, adapted from *Business,* 7th ed., by William M. Pride, Robert J. Hughes, and Jack R. Kapoor (Houghton Mifflin Company, 2002, p. 360); **page 90:** Global Smoking graphic: "Global Smoking," World Health Organization, November 21, 2003 (http://www.cnn.com/HEALTH/9704/16/tobacco.world/); **page 90:** Photo, Advertisement for Cigarettes, © Getty Images.

Chapter 9: page 91: © Jose Luis Pelaez, Inc./Corbis; **page 92:** Reading, "The Economics of Diamonds and Water," adapted from *Fundamentals of Economics,* 2nd. ed., by William Boyes and Michael Melvin (Houghton Mifflin Company, 2003, pp. 3–4); **page 99:** © Royalty-Free/Corbis.

Chapter 10: page 101: © Jose Luis Pelaez, Inc./Corbis; **page 103:** Reading, "The Changing Roles of Men and Women in the Workplace," adapted from *Business,* 7th ed., by William M. Pride, Robert J. Hughes, and Jack R. Kapoor (Houghton Mifflin Company, 2002, p. 310).

Chapter 11: page 107, clockwise from upper left: © David Young-Wolff/PhotoEdit; © Michael Newman/PhotoEdit; © Patrick Olear/PhotoEdit; © Cathrine Wesset/Corbis; **page 108:** Reading, "Innate and Cultural Influences on Emotional Expressions," adapted from *Psychology,* 6th ed., by Douglas A. Bernstein, Louis A. Penner, Allison Clarke-Stewart, and Edward J. Roy (Houghton Mifflin Company, 2003, pp. 425–427); **page 118:** Speaking, "Conducting a Survey," from "The Recognition of Threatening Facial Stimuli," by J. Aronoff, A. M. Barclay, and L. A. Stevenson, the *Journal of Personality and Social Psychology,* 54, 1988, p. 651. Copyright 1988 by the American Psychological Association. Adapted with permission.

Chapter 12: page 120: © Corbis; **page 121:** Reading, "The Impact of the Industrial Revolution," adapted from *The Earth and Its Peoples: A Global History,* 2nd ed, by Richard W. Bulliet, Pamela Kyle Crossley, Daniel R. Headrick, Steven W. Hirsch, Lyman J. Johnson, and David Northrup (Houghton Mifflin, 2003, p. 471).

Chapter 13: page 131: © www.CartoonStock.com; **page 132:** Reading, "Political Campaigns and the Media," adapted from *The Human Polity: A Comparative Introduction to Political Science,* 5th ed., by Kay Lawson (Houghton Mifflin, 2003, pp. 239–241, 248–249).

Chapter 14: page 143: © Bettman/Corbis; **page 144:** Reading, "Can Non-Humans Use Language?" adapted from *Psychology,* 6th ed., by Douglas A. Bernstein, Louis A. Penner, Allison Clarke-Stewart, and Edward J. Roy (Houghton Mifflin, 2003, pp. 301–303); **page 152:** Speaking, "Linguistic Analysis," graphic from *Psychology,* 6th ed., by Douglas A. Bernstein, Louis A. Penner, Allison Clarke-Stewart, and Edward J. Roy (Houghton Mifflin, 2003, p. 294).

Chapter 15: page 154: © Bob Daemmrich; **page 155:** Close Reading, "Lie Detection Tests," adapted from *Psychology,* 6th ed., by Douglas A. Bernstein, Louis A. Penner, Allison Clarke-Stewart, and Edward J. Roy (Houghton Mifflin, 2003, pp. 420–421).

Chapter 16: page 160: © Joseph Sohm; ChromoSohm Inc./Corbis, © Royalty-Free/Corbis; **page 161:** Reading, "Renewable Alternative Energy Resources," adapted from *Earth: Geologic Principles and History,* by Stanley Chernicoff, Haydn A. "Chip" Fox, and Lawrence H. Tanner (Houghton Mifflin, 2002, pp. 360–363).

Chapter 17: page 174: © Dutheil Didier/Corbis Sygma; **page 175:** Reading, "What Caused the Extinction of the Dinosaurs?" adapted from *Earth: Geologic Principles and History,* by Stanley Chernicoff, Haydn A. "Chip" Fox, and Lawrence H. Tanner (Houghton Mifflin, 2002, pp. 4–5).

Chapter 18: page 185: © Steve Chenn/Corbis; **page 186:** Reading, "Chemistry Facts: The Good, the Bad, and the *Odd,*" adapted from *An Introduction to Physical Science,* 10th ed., by James T. Shipman, Jerry D. Wilson, and Aaron W. Todd (Houghton Mifflin, 2003, pp. 310–311, 328–329); **page 194:** Photo, Antoine-Laurent de Lavoisier, © Getty Images; **page 196:** Speaking, Explaining a Chemistry Concept (Figure 13.20), "pH Scale Diagram" adapted from *An Introduction to Physical Science,* 10th ed., by James T. Shipman, Jerry D. Wilson, and Aaron W. Todd (Houghton Mifflin, 2003, p. 332); "Some Common Bases" and "Some Common Acids" © Runk/Schoenberger/Grant Heilman Photography.

Chapter 19: page 199: © Dex Images/Corbis; **page 200:** Reading, "Privacy in the Digital Age" adapted from *Media Today: An Introduction to Mass Communication*, 2nd ed., by Joseph Turow (Houghton Mifflin, 2003, pp. 529–532).

Chapter 20: page 212: © Richard Hutchings/PhotoEdit; **page 213:** Cloze Reading, "Understanding Speech," adapted from *Psychology*, 6th ed., by Douglas A. Bernstein, Louis A. Penner, Allison Clarke-Stewart, and Edward J. Roy (Houghton Mifflin, 2003, pp. 294–295); **page 220:** Vocabulary in Context, "The Online Privacy Crisis" adapted from *Americans Online Privacy: The System Is Broken. A Report from the Annenberg Public Policy Center of the University of Pennsylvania*, by Joseph Turow (http://www.appcpenn.org/ 04_info_society/2003_online_privacy_version_09.pdf; June 2003).

Appendix I: page 221: "The Dictionary Entry: Elements of the Dictionary" from *The American Heritage English as a Second Language Dictionary Workbook*, by Ann Silverman (Houghton Mifflin, 1999, p. 3).

Appendix VI: page 237: Words from the Academic Word List, compiled by Averil Coxhead (http://www.vuw .ac.nz/lals/staff/averil-coxhead/awl/index.html; A.Coxhead@massey.ac.nz)

All dictionary excerpts in the text are from *The American Heritage English as a Second Language Dictionary* (Houghton Mifflin, 1998).

LEARNING STYLES

WORD LIST

Noun		Verb	Adjective
analysis	issue	assume	available
approach	method	edit	cooperative
area	period	establish	economic
benefit	process	identify	major
concept	research	indicate	significant
data	role	involve	similar
evidence	structure	occur	specific
factor	team		theoretical
formula	thesis		
individual	variables		
interpretation			

PREVIEW QUESTIONS

1. What are the people in the photograph probably doing?

2. What is meant by cooperative learning?

3. Have you ever done a project or an assignment in a cooperative learning group? Describe your experience.

4. What are the advantages of cooperative learning? What are the disadvantages?

5. How could cooperative learning help you learn vocabulary?

6. What is your preferred learning style?

READING

COOPERATIVE LEARNING

1   The **cooperative** learning **approach** has become popular among college professors because it helps students reach high academic standards and build positive relationships in the classroom. After many years of **theoretical** and practical **research** on this **issue**, strong **evidence** shows that cooperative **methods** can have **major benefits** for student learning through increased learning,
5   better understanding of the **concepts** being taught, and improved retention of the material. In addition, an **interpretation** of **available data** suggests that cooperative learning encourages positive relationships among **team** members of different racial and **economic** backgrounds.

Cooperative learning takes a variety of forms, but the **structure** of most cooperative learning **involves** small teams, usually composed of four or five **individuals,** working together toward a
10   **similar** goal in which each person **assumes** a **specific role** in the **process** over a **period** of time. Cooperative groups might be **established** for one class session or for several weeks to complete a specific assignment. Students are expected to interact with members of their group, share ideas and materials, support and encourage each other's academic learning, explain to each other the concepts of the assignment, and make sure that each individual is responsible for doing a fair
15   share of the work.

Analyses of the cooperative approach have **identified** several **significant factors** and **variables** that **indicate** a **formula** for successful cooperative learning to **occur.** Studies have shown that students on successful teams interact with a higher level of language, ask each other difficult questions, challenge each other's answers, and ask each other for assistance. College classes in all
20   **areas** of study are likely to involve some type of cooperative learning, from peer **editing** of **thesis** statements and review of essays in writing courses to long-term group projects in the sciences. This approach to learning is generally more interesting and more fun for students than traditional classroom teaching, although problems can arise when the team members do not cooperate with each other.

Key Elements of Successful Cooperative Learning: **http://www.cde.ca.gov/iasa/cooplrng2.html.** Adapted from Eugene Garcia, *Student Cultural Diversity: Understanding and Meeting the Challenge,* 3rd ed. (Boston: Houghton Mifflin Company, 2002), 344–45.

1. VOCABULARY IN CONTEXT

Choose the best meaning according to the context in which the word is used in the reading.

a.	**approach** (line 1)	situation	<u>method</u>	movement
b.	**evidence** (line 3)	research	proof	crime
c.	**benefits** (line 4)	advantages	insurance	social events
d.	**concepts** (line 5)	ideas	meanings	generalizations
e.	**interpretation** (line 6)	version	translation	explanation
f.	**structure** (line 8)	arrangement	building	schedule
g.	**involves** (line 9)	invites	participates	includes
h.	**role** (line 10)	wheel	movement	part
i.	**period** (line 10)	century	duration	punctuation mark
j.	**significant** (line 16)	obvious	important	similar
k.	**variables** (line 16)	quantities	varieties	variations

2. READING COMPREHENSION

2A Getting the Facts

Put a check mark (✓) next to each statement that is an effective strategy for successful cooperative learning.

a. _____ collaboration among team members

b. _____ emphasis on individual achievement

c. _____ fair division of responsibility for the assignment

d. _____ similar goals among team members

e. _____ primary concern for the individual's grade

f. _____ clear communication among members

g. _____ individual decision making

h. _____ discussion of concepts being learned

i. _____ support and encouragement among members

j. _____ competition among group members

k. _____ friendly relationships among group members

l. _____ leadership of the group by one person

Your motivation to increase your knowledge of academic vocabulary is an important factor in learning the words effectively.

2B Making Inferences

Apply the information you have read about cooperative learning to infer the answers to the following questions.

1. What benefits do you think students can gain from cooperative learning?

   _____

   _____

2. Why do you think that students from different backgrounds form better relationships with each other when they work together?

   _____

   _____

3. What teamwork skills are needed to work in a group?

   _____

   _____

4. What factors may influence the success of a cooperative group?

   _____

   _____

5. Describe a possible cooperative learning activity for one of the classes you are taking now.

   _____

   _____

3. DICTIONARY SKILLS

Study the dictionary entry for *issue*. Read the following sentences and give the dictionary definition of each underlined word.

> **is•sue** (ĭsh′o͞o) *n.* **1.** [C] A subject being discussed; a question under debate: *the issue of reforming campaign laws.* **2.** [C] Something, especially printed, that is distributed or put into circulation: *a new issue of postage stamps; the June issue of the magazine.* **3.** [U] **a.** The act of flowing out, or a place of outflow: *the issue of water from the spring; a lake with no issue to the sea.* **b.** The act of distributing or putting out; release: *The date of issue is on the front of the newspaper.* —*v.* **is•sued, is•su•ing, is•sues.** —*intr.* To come out; flow out: *Water issued from the broken pipe.* —*tr.* **1.** To put (sthg.) in circulation; publish: *The Postal Service issues stamps.* **2.** To give (sthg.) out; distribute: *The school will issue uniforms to members of the team.* **3.** To cause (sthg.) to flow out: *The factory issues its waste water into tanks for treatment.* ♦ **at issue.** Being discussed or questioned: *Your conduct is not at issue here.* **take issue with.** To disagree with (sbdy./sthg.): *He took issue with my view of the problem.* —**is′su•ance** *n.* [U] **-is′su•er** *n.*

1. The December <u>issue</u> of *Newsweek* features an article on the study
   habits of university students.   _____

2. The program <u>issues</u> certificates to all students who successfully
    complete the course.   _____

3. Students usually enjoy discussing class <u>issues</u> together.   _____

4. Dan's professor <u>took issue with</u> his argument in his term paper. _____

5. The topic of today's geology lecture was the <u>issue</u> of water from rivers
    into oceans.   _____

6. Information about study groups <u>was issued</u> to all members of the class. _____

7. <u>At issue</u> in this meeting are the activities that promote cooperative
    learning.   _____

8. I'm looking for a journal with the <u>date of issue</u> January 2005.   _____

4. WORD FORMS

4A Chart Completion

Complete the chart below with the different forms of each word. An X indicates that there is no
word form.

Noun	Verb	Adjective	Adverb
analysis	analyze	analytic, analytical	analytically
concept			
		economic	
formula			X
	identify		
individual			
		major	X
	occur	X	X
period	X		
		specific	
	edit		

4B Word Forms in Sentences

Use the correct word form from the chart in the previous exercise to complete the following sentences. Make sure the word you choose fits meaningfully and grammatically into the sentence.

1. analysis   Scientists always ____*analyze*____ their data before writing up the results of their research.

2. concept   We _____ the idea for the project after discussing it in our group.

3. economic   Our ability to find a good job after graduation will depend to some extent on the strength of the _____.

4. formula   We are encouraged by our professors to _____ and express our own opinions.

5. identify   You need two forms of personal _____.

6. individual   Although the members of our study group have _____ learning styles, we all work well together.

7. major   Most students change their _____ at least once during their undergraduate studies.

8. occur   There was a strange _____ in the dorm last night when all the lights suddenly went out.

9. period   It is normal for first-year students to experience _____ homesickness during their first semester away from home.

10. specific   Our professor _____ said to turn in the assignment on Thursday.

11. edit   Students often find it difficult to understand their classmates' _____ comments when they are peer reviewing an essay.

5. COLLOCATIONS

The following nouns are commonly found with specific verbs and adjectives.

Verbs	Adjectives	Noun
carry out, do, make, perform, conduct	careful, brief, detailed, theoretical, economic, financial	**analysis**
find, provide, come up with, discover, use	complicated, simple, correct, mathematical, scientific, successful, traditional	**formula**
gain, reap, obtain, receive, provide, offer	considerable, enormous, great, major, economic, maximum, substantial	**benefit**
understand, define, formulate, introduce, develop	general, basic, simple, theoretical, scientific, economic, intellectual	**concept**
collect, gather, store, record, analyze, study, process, interpret	accurate, statistical, numerical, environmental, financial, economic	**data**

Complete each sentence with an appropriate verb, adjective, or noun from the previous chart. More than one answer is possible.

1. Students can _____*gain*_____ considerable benefits from learning to work together.

2. Our assignment was to define the _____ concepts in Chapter 10 of the textbook.

3. Our group project is to study environmental _____ on annual rainfall in our state.

4. I could not find the _____ formula to complete this calculation.

5. When Bill performed a _____ analysis of his project, he realized that he had made a mistake.

6. In our first class, the professor introduced the _____ concepts of the course.

7. In our group project for Business 101, we have to _____ the financial data of a major company.

8. We should carry out a _____ analysis of the topic before we spend a lot of time on it.

9. I expect to gain _____ benefits from my degree program.

10. Our group found a successful _____ for identifying the chemicals.

6. WORD PARTS

vis/vid (see)

6A Each of the following words contains the word part *vis* or *vid*, Latin words that mean "see." In each word notice the word part that gives a clue about the word's meaning. Match each word with its meaning.

1.	_g_	ev**id**ence	**a.** change the original version
2.	____	in**vis**ible	**b.** a device for seeing images on a screen
3.	____	re**vis**e	**c.** the state of being visible
4.	____	super**vis**or	**d.** the sense of sight
5.	____	tele**vis**ion	**e.** relating to the sense of sight
6.	____	**vid**eo	**f.** person in charge
7.	____	**vis**ibility	**g.** facts that show the truth
8.	____	**vis**ion	**h.** a person who visits
9.	____	**vis**itor	**i.** form a mental picture
10.	____	**vis**ual	**j.** impossible to see
11.	____	**vis**ualize	**k.** the visual part of a broadcast

6B The following common collocations have specific meanings. Complete each sentence with the appropriate collocation.

visual aid	visually impaired
visiting hours	visiting professor
poor visibility	visible to the naked eye
20/20 vision	visitation rights

1. The fog created very _poor visibility_ on the highway this morning, forcing vehicles to drive very slowly and carefully.

2. When her parents got divorced, Janet went to live with her father, but her mother had _____.

3. I can only visit my grandmother during _____ at the hospital.

4. Our geography professor always uses some type of _____ in class to make the lectures more interesting.

5. Although bacteria are not _____, they can be identified under a microscope.

6. Our _____ from China, who has given several excellent lectures about Chinese history, will be returning home next semester.

7. My glasses give me _____, but without them I can hardly see anything.

8. Guide dogs are trained to help the _____ safely travel around the city.

7. WRITING

7A Paraphrasing

See *Appendix III* for additional information on paraphrasing.

Match the original text in the first column to the paraphrase of the text in the second column. Notice how words and grammar structures change in the paraphrase, yet the meaning remains the same.

Original Text

1. The cooperative learning approach has become popular among college professors because it helps students reach high academic standards.

2. Strong evidence shows that cooperative methods can have major benefits for student learning.

3. An interpretation of available data suggests that cooperative learning encourages positive relationships among team members of different racial and economic backgrounds.

4. Cooperative groups might be established for one class session or for several weeks to complete a specific assignment.

5. College classes in all areas of study are likely to involve some type of cooperative learning.

6. Problems can arise when the team members do not cooperate with each other.

Paraphrase

a. __6__ *Students who do not work well with each other in their groups may cause difficulties.*

b. _____ *It is evident that students can greatly improve their learning experience by working with other students.*

c. _____ *College students can improve their academic performance in classes taught by faculty who encourage methods of collaborative learning.*

d. _____ *Some kind of team learning will probably occur in every subject studied at a university.*

e. _____ *According to research studies, team projects promote better understanding among students from different backgrounds and cultures.*

f. _____ *A particular class project might require a team of students to cooperate for one or more class meetings.*

7B Paragraph Writing

Write a response to **one** of the following topics. Include at least **six to eight vocabulary words** in your paragraph.

1. Describe an experience when you worked with others on a project. Describe the benefits and the negative aspects of working cooperatively. In what ways did you learn more about the topic and about your teammates?

2. Read the e-mail that Maria sent to her friend Alicia about the course requirements for a psychology class. Write a response to Maria in the format and style of an e-mail, giving her advice on how to get her team members to cooperate equally on their group project so that they can all get a good grade.

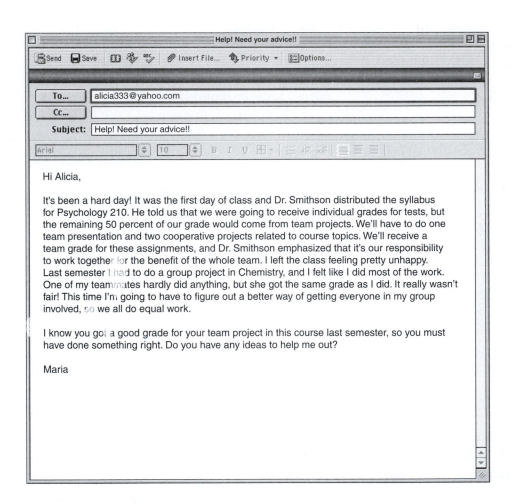

Hi Alicia,

It's been a hard day! It was the first day of class and Dr. Smithson distributed the syllabus for Psychology 210. He told us that we were going to receive individual grades for tests, but the remaining 50 percent of our grade would come from team projects. We'll have to do one team presentation and two cooperative projects related to course topics. We'll receive a team grade for these assignments, and Dr. Smithson emphasized that it's our responsibility to work together for the benefit of the whole team. I left the class feeling pretty unhappy. Last semester I had to do a group project in Chemistry, and I felt like I did most of the work. One of my teammates hardly did anything, but she got the same grade as I did. It really wasn't fair! This time I'm going to have to figure out a better way of getting everyone in my group involved, so we all do equal work.

I know you got a good grade for your team project in this course last semester, so you must have done something right. Do you have any ideas to help me out?

Maria

8. SPEAKING

8A Group Discussion: Study Locations

Students like to study in different places and at different times, alone or in a group, with noise or music in the background or in a quiet natural environment. Take turns describing your favorite place to study. Include details about its environment, its atmosphere and location, and the comforts of the place of study. Prepare a short oral summary of these favorite study locations to present to the whole class.

8B Pair Discussion: Learning Styles Analysis

Students enter college with a variety of learning styles. The most common styles are visual, auditory, and tactile/kinesthetic learning styles. It is important to be aware of your learning style so that you can perform at your best in the different types of courses and exams that you will experience in college.

There are several websites where you can analyze your own learning style by answering a number of questions. Using *Learning Styles Survey* or *Learning Styles Questionnaire* as the keyword, search for an appropriate website and complete the survey. Analyze the results of the questionnaire, focusing on the questions below. Discuss what you learned about your own learning style with a partner.

- According to the survey, what kind of learning style do you have?

- Do you agree with the results?

- Did you learn anything new about your own learning style?

- Why do you think you have developed this learning style?

- What kind of teaching style or learning environment matches your learning style?

- How will your own learning style influence the kinds of courses you take in college?

- How do you prefer to study for tests?

- Would you like to change your learning style in any way? If so, what would you change and how could you do it?

Address: http://elt.heinle.com/essentialvocab ▸ go

For more activities related to this chapter, go to the *Essential Academic Vocabulary* website.

STRESS IN COLLEGE LIFE

WORD LIST

Noun		Verb	Adjective
assistance	potential	achieve	academic
context	psychologist	consult	appropriate
depression	range	create	classic
environment	section	define	conducive
error	sector	derive	consistent
function	source	estimate	financial
income	stress	impact	legal
item	text	license	parallel
percent	welfare	relax	tense
		require	
		respond	
		seek	

PREVIEW QUESTIONS

1. How do you think the students in the photograph are feeling?

2. Have you ever experienced test anxiety? How did you feel?

3. How can students reduce test anxiety?

4. What was the most important exam you have ever taken? How did you manage the stress associated with it?

5. What other types of stress do students often experience?

6. What has been your most stressful experience this semester? How did you deal with it?

7. What advice would you give to a student who seems unable to function because of high levels of stress?

READING

TEST ANXIETY

1
- "I really studied for this test, but when I got in the room, I couldn't remember a thing."

- "When I looked at the first **section** and couldn't answer any of the **items**, I knew I was going to make all kinds of **errors**."

- "I'm always afraid of exams because I never do well."

5
- "I'm so **tense**, my hands sweat. I can't think, and when I look around, everybody is working away but me. I just can't **relax**!"

- "When I read a **text** in a test situation, I can't remember what I've read."

These statements reflect how some students **respond** to test anxiety. Test anxiety is **stress** related to testing. Stress is **defined** as the body's response to an important occurrence or event.
10 The event in this **context** is the combination of the test preparation and the test itself. On the one hand, a little anxiety is **conducive** to performance. On the other hand, when the stress level is too high, it may **impact** memory, creating in the student a loss of **function** in testing **environments** with **parallel** negative effects on his or her **welfare**.

About fifty **percent** of students experience test anxiety at some point in their college years.
15 However, test anxiety is only one of a **range** of stresses experienced by college students on a daily basis. In the college **sector**, some of the **classic sources** of stress **derive** from the **academic** environment and relationships with friends and roommates. Major life changes, such as changes in **income** level or **legal** and **financial** issues, can also **create** mental and physical feelings of stress and anxiety, which can overload the ability to function well.

20 Stress can also result from students' own unrealistic expectations. When students **require** too much of themselves by **overestimating** their abilities, they may fail to **achieve** their goals or to make **consistent** progress towards them. Failure also creates tensions that have the **potential** to

produce a state of **depression** for which students may need to **seek appropriate assistance** by **consulting** a **psychologist** or other **licensed** professional.

———————

Adapted from T. Anne Hawkins, *Connections: Orientation 1,* 2nd ed. (Morgantown, WV: West Virginia University, 2000), 169, 176–77.

1. VOCABULARY IN CONTEXT

Determine how the boldface words are used in the reading. Then for each item, choose the word or phrase that is closest in meaning.

1. __*b*__ **impact** (line 12)

   a. hit against something

   b. have an effect

   c. make an identification

2. _____ **function** (line 12)

   a. a formal social gathering

   b. benefit

   c. normal activity of something

3. _____ **sources** (line 16)

   a. point of beginning

   b. research documentation

   c. variables

4. _____ **environment** (line 13)

   a. nature

   b. surroundings

   c. interpretation

5. _____ **income** (line 18)

   a. arrival

   b. employment

   c. money

6. _____ **create** (line 18)

   a. produce

   b. approach

   c. specify

7. _____ **require** (line 20)

   a. involve

   b. assume

   c. demand

8. _____ **overestimating** (line 21)

   a. establishing

   b. rating too low

   c. rating too highly

9. _____ **potential** (line 22)

   a. capacity

   b. strength

   c. influence

10. _____ **appropriate** (line 23)

   a. individual

   b. significant

   c. suitable

11. _____ **assistance** (line 23)

   a. aid

   b. analysis

   c. involvement

2. READING COMPREHENSION

2A Getting the Facts

According to the text, students who suffer from test anxiety experience a variety of classic symptoms. Put a check mark (✔) next to each symptom of test anxiety described in the text.

a. _____ loss of sleep

b. _____ depression

c. _____ fear of tests

d. _____ inability to function

e. _____ loss of income

f. _____ increased errors

g. _____ loss of memory

h. _____ extreme nervousness

i. _____ sweaty hands

j. _____ inability to remember written texts

k. _____ overestimation of skills

l. _____ increased energy

2B Making Inferences

Apply the information you have read about *academic stress* to infer the answers to the following statements.

1. From your experience, name **four** types of *academic stress* that might affect typical college students.

   a. _____

   b. _____

   c. _____

   d. _____

2. Name **four** *major life changes* that might create stressful conditions for students.

   a. _____

   b. _____

   c. _____

   d. _____

> Individualize strategies for learning and reviewing vocabulary. Practice various methods until you discover the strategies that work for you.

3. Name **four** *unrealistic expectations* that college students might have.

   a. _____

   b. _____

   c. _____

   d. _____

4. Students who suffer from severe stress or depression may need to *seek appropriate professional assistance.* Who should they consult?

   _____

3. DICTIONARY SKILLS

Study the dictionary entry for *range*. Complete the following sentences with the appropriate phrases below.

range (rānj) *n.* **1.** [U] The extent of or area covered by sthg.: *within viewing range; the range of his interests.* **2.** [C] An extent or amount of difference: *a price range.* **3.** [C] An extended group or series, especially a row or chain of mountains: *a mountain range; a wide range of products.* **4.** [C] The area in which a kind of animal or plant normally lives or grows. **5.** [U] A large expanse of open land on which livestock wander and graze: *cowboys riding across the range.* **6.** [C] The greatest distance of operation, as of a sound, radio signal, or missile: *a radio receiver with a range of 200 miles.* **7.** [C] A place for practice in shooting at targets: *a firing range.* **8.** [C] A stove with spaces for cooking a number of things at the same time: *an electric range.* —*intr.v.* **ranged, rang•ing, rang•es. 1.** To vary or move between specified limits: *children whose ages ranged from four to ten.* **2.** To extend in a certain direction: *a river ranging westward.* **3.** To live or grow within a certain region: *Coyotes now range over the entire United States.*

viewing range	range of symptoms	price range
mountain range	firing range	open range
gas range	age range	within normal range
range of products	out of range	

1. The ___age range___ in this class varies from 17 to 34.

2. When my car broke down on the highway, I could not call for help on my cell phone because it was _____.

3. The Himalayas are the most famous _____ in the world.

4. My mother always cooks on a _____.

5. Test anxiety can produce a _____, from an inability to sleep to depression.

6. In the American West, cowboys still ride their horses on the _____.

7. Before the beginning of hunting season, many hunters like to practice shooting at a _____.

8. My sister was pleased that the results of her recent medical tests were _____.

9. At first, I thought the animal was a bear, but when it came within _____, I could see that it was just a big dog.

10. Last weekend I went shopping for shoes, but I could not find any I liked in my _____.

11. The Kodak Company makes a _____ for photography.

4. WORD FORMS

4A Chart Completion

Complete the chart with the corresponding noun or verb forms.

Noun	Verb
assistance	assist
	achieve
conduct	
	create
definition	
	estimate
function	
	require
item	
	impact
range	
	consult
response	

4B Word Forms in Sentences

Create five new sentences about test anxiety or stress, using a noun and a verb from the chart in the previous exercise in each sentence.

1. _Students who are impacted by test anxiety can receive professional assistance._
2. _____
3. _____
4. _____
5. _____
6. _____

5. COLLOCATIONS

5A The following nouns are typically found in combination with specific verbs. Match the nouns with the verbs to make meaningful phrases.

speed	advice	shelter	cost	size	assistance

estimate _____size_____   seek _____

_____   _____

_____   _____

problems	benefit	satisfaction	jobs	pleasure	poems

create _____   derive _____

_____   _____

_____   _____

5B Match the situations in the following sentences with the collocations that describe them.

financial assistance	disorderly conduct
a friendly environment	a university function
welfare state	licensed psychologist
yearly income	the sports section
legal issues	achievement test

1. ___disorderly conduct___ The judge convicted the middle-aged man for public drunkenness and aggressive behavior.

2. _____ My father always reads the news about football and baseball first.

3. _____ Lawyers are required to be experts in matters of law.

4. _____ We enjoy living in this area because the people are welcoming and always give us assistance when we need it.

5. _____ Federal taxes are based on the amount of money earned in a 12-month period.

6. _____ Next week I must attend an important evening event with the professors in my department.

7. _____ At the end of our Spanish course, we took an exam to find out how much we had learned.

8. _____ Many students need to apply for a loan in order to pay college tuition.

9. _____ Many European countries provide free medical care and other benefits to all citizens.

10. _____ A college counselor must take special tests to become certified to practice psychology.

6. WORD PARTS

Negative Prefixes

The most common English negative prefix for adjectives is _un-_ (e.g., _unhappy_, _unkind_, _unpopular_), which means _not_. Other negative prefixes include _il-_, _ir-_, _im-_, _in-_, and _non-_. Some of these negative prefixes are used predictably, while others have no rules and have to be individually learned.

Prefix	Rule	Example
ir-	before _r_	irrelevant, irresponsible
il-	before _l_	illicit, illogical
im-	before _p, b, m_	imperfect, immoral
in-	all others	incomplete, inexcusable
un-	(no rule)	uncomfortable, unpredictable
non-	(no rule)	nonalcoholic, nonsmoking
dis-	(no rule)	disagreeable, disconnect

Change the meanings of the following adjectives by adding a negative prefix.

1. accurate _inaccurate_

2. available _____

3. complete _____

4. constitutional _____

5. involved _____

6. mature _____

7. regular _____

8. significant _____

9. stop _____

10. licensed _____

11. appropriate _____

12. similar _____

13. consistent _____

14. dependent _____

15. legal _____

16. necessary _____

17. resident _____

18. satisfied _____

19. variable _____

20. cooperative _____

7. WRITING

7A Writing a Summary

See *Appendix IV* for additional information on summarizing.

Find an article about test anxiety on the Internet. (Most major universities have information on their websites.) Take notes in your own words about the main ideas in the text and use these notes to summarize the information. Include and underline at least **six to eight vocabulary words** in your summary.

7B Paragraph Writing

Write a response to **one** of the following topics. Include at least **six to eight vocabulary words** in your paragraph.

1. Describe an experience when you felt a great deal of anxiety about a test. Why was this test important? What physical symptoms did you have? What was the outcome of the test? How could you have relieved your test anxiety?

2. Describe another major stress that college students often experience, such as stress related to roommates, romance, family, career, or health. How does this stress affect academic performance and students' personal lives? What are some ways that students can deal effectively with this type of stress?

8. SPEAKING

8A Partner Discussion: Stress Reduction Methods

Discuss with your partner the following methods that people can use to reduce stress. Which ones do you find helpful? Which ones have you never tried? What other stress reduction activities can you add to the list?

breathing exercises	meditation	positive self-talk
body relaxation	sleep	journal writing
massage	talking to friends	listening to music
yoga	physical exercise	time management

8B Role-Plays

Using new words from this chapter, act out the following role-plays.

1. Your friend is becoming very nervous about the final exam in chemistry. He has had problems with test anxiety in the past, and he is afraid that he will forget everything as soon as he walks in the door of the examination room. Advise your friend about what he should do to minimize test anxiety.

2. It has been a difficult semester for you. Your long-term girlfriend/boyfriend broke up with you, and you are failing one of your classes. You are feeling so stressed out that you decide to seek assistance from the college counseling center. Tell the counselor what kinds of stress you have been experiencing and what you have been doing to try to relax more. Ask the counselor for some advice in dealing better with your problems and with your stress level.

Address: http://elt.heinle.com/essentialvocab   ▶ go

For more activities related to this chapter, go to the *Essential Academic Vocabulary* website.

STUDENT HOUSING

WORD LIST

Noun		Verb	Adjective
administration	maintenance	assess	final
aspect	orientation	evaluate	institutional
community	policy	obtain	positive
computer	regulation	perceive	primary
construction	security	purchase	
contract	site	reside	
design	strategy	restrict	
distribution	transfer	select	
element	utility	survey	
labor			

PREVIEW QUESTIONS

1. What is your housing situation now? Where do you live and with whom?

2. Do you prefer to live alone or with a roommate? Why?

3. What are the advantages of living in a college dormitory? What are the disadvantages?

4. Why do many students prefer to live off campus?

5. In addition to paying rent for an apartment, what other expenses might you have?

6. What is a lease? Why do renters have to sign one?

6. What do you think you would learn if you attended a housing orientation on campus?

READING

RENTAL BASICS

1 Most first-year college students live in **institutional** housing, such as a dormitory or an apartment building. However, most second-year and **transfer** students are ready to move into off-campus housing and take on the responsibilities of living in a rental unit. However, there are certain **aspects** of renting that students should keep in mind before **selecting** a housing option.

5   First, it will be beneficial to visit the campus housing assistance center to attend an **orientation** on issues such as landlord/tenant rights, legal **contracts**, and roommate matching services. Participants will also learn **strategies** for the housing search. Students should carefully **assess** the type of **community** in which they want to **reside** and the type of housing they want. Some housing units have many **regulations** for **residents,** which students may **perceive** as

10 unnecessary, while their units may have **construction** or **design elements** that **restrict** students' comfort and convenience. Before signing the lease, it is important to **obtain** a complete tour of the housing unit from the **administration** in order to **survey** the facilities and the condition of the rental unit. Potential renters should **evaluate** the answers to the following questions before making a **final** decision:

15 • Which **utilities** are included in the rent?

• Who does the **maintenance** on the apartment?

• Who pays for the **labor** on repairs?

• What kind of **computer** access is available?

• What is the **distribution** of students and the general public living in the apartment
20 building?

• Are there **on-site** fitness facilities?

• What kinds of **security** systems are in use?

• Are there any restrictions regarding smoking?

• What are the **policies** regarding pets?

25 • How much is the security deposit?

- Is free parking available?

- Who is the **primary** contact for residents in case of an emergency?

- Is the renter required to **purchase** additional rental insurance?

Finally, students should make sure they find financially responsible roommates. A landlord
30 can legally hold the other tenants responsible if one cotenant fails to make the rental payments or
moves out. However, students should have **positive** experiences if they have realistic expectations
of their roommates and their landlord.

1. VOCABULARY IN CONTEXT

Determine how the words in column A are used in the reading. Then choose the word in column
B that is closest in meaning.

Column A	Column B
1. _____ institutional (line 1)	a. assess
2. _____ select (line 4)	b. buy
3. _____ contract (line 6)	c. first
4. _____ strategy (line 7)	d. person
5. _____ community (line 8)	e. college
6. _____ resident (line 9)	f. feature
7. _____ element (line 10)	g. tenant
8. _____ obtain (line 11)	h. area
9. _____ survey (line 12)	i. safety
10. _____ evaluate (line 13)	j. choose
11. _____ security (line 22)	k. receive
12. _____ policies (line 24)	l. inspect
13. _____ primary (line 27)	m. lease
14. _____ contact (line 27)	n. regulations
15. _____ purchase (line 28)	o. method

2. READING COMPREHENSION

2A Getting the Facts

Put a check mark (✓) next to each item mentioned in the text that a person should consider before deciding to rent an apartment.

a. _____ safety

b. _____ responsible roommates

c. _____ parking space

d. _____ spa and swimming pool

e. _____ animal regulations

f. _____ exercise facilities

g. _____ nearby shopping center

h. _____ rules about late-night parties

i. _____ restrictions on overnight visitors

j. _____ helpful administration

k. _____ laundry facilities

l. _____ responsibility for repairs

m. _____ rental insurance

n. _____ payment of a deposit

o. _____ type of neighborhood

p. _____ Internet access

q. _____ regulations about noise

r. _____ cost of gas, electricity, and water

s. _____ smoking regulations

t. _____ apartment design

2B Making Inferences

Apply the information you read about the basics of renting to infer answers to the following questions.

1. What type of community would a student probably prefer to live in?

   _____

   _____

2. What kinds of housing regulations might students dislike?

   _____

   _____

3. Name three responsibilities that students might have as renters that they would not have living in a dormitory.

   _____

   _____

4. List three strategies for finding appropriate housing.

   _____

   _____

> Be aware of what it means to *know* a word. Use a dictionary to find information about words, such as word forms and different meanings.

5. Give several examples of realistic expectations of roommates.

_____

_____

6. What might happen if one roommate moves out of a rental unit before the end of the lease?

_____

_____

3. DICTIONARY SKILLS

Study the dictionary entries for *administer, administration,* and *administrative.* Read the following sentences and fill in the blanks below with the correct words.

ad•min•is•ter   (ăd mĭn′ĭ stər) *tr.v.* **1.** To manage or direct the affairs of (sthg.): *The mayor administers the city government.* **2.a.** To give out or dispense (sthg.): *A doctor administers medicine.* **b.** To give and supervise (sthg.): *administer a test.* **3.** To give (sthg.) formally or officially: *administer an oath of office.*
ad•min•is•tra•tion   (ăd mĭn′ĭ stra–′shən) *n.* **1.** [U] The act or process of directing the affairs of a business, school, or other institution; management. **2.** [U] The people who manage an institution or direct an organization: *The school administration is made up of the principal and a staff of teachers.* **3.** [C; U] Often **Administration.** The executive branch of a government, especially the President of the United States and the cabinet. **4.** [C] The time that a chief executive is in office or that a government is in power: *Many civil rights laws were enacted during President Johnson's administration.* **5.** [U] The act of administering: *administration of justice; administration of an oath.* **-ad•min′is•trate** (ăd mĭ′n′ĭˇ strāt′) *v.*
ad•min•is•tra•tive   (ăd mĭ′n′ĭ strā′tĭv *or* ăd mĭ′n′ĭ strə tĭv) *adj.* Relating to government or management: *a manager with administrative ability; the President and other administrative officers of the government.* **-ad•min′is•tra′tive•ly** *adv.*

1. Who is the person most likely to be responsible for the administration of the following?

    a. a test   _____

    b. a business   _____

    c. a school   _____

    d. an apartment building   _____

    e. an academic department _____

    f. cough medicine   _____

    g. government   _____

    h. justice   _____

    i. painkillers   _____

    j. a city   _____

2. List four administrative activities for which an apartment manager would be responsible.

a. _____   c. _____

b. _____   d. _____

3. List four qualities of a good administrator.

a. _____   c. _____

b. _____   d. _____

4. WORD FORMS IN SENTENCES

Complete the following sentences using the grammatically correct form of the word in italics. (It may be necessary to change a verb form or tense or to make a noun plural.)

1. The job as housing supervisor requires excellent _____ skills.

administration, administer, administrative, administratively

2. The housing advisor _____ information about leases at the housing orientation.

distribution, distribute

3. This year, most of my friends _____ in off-campus housing.

residence, reside, residential

4. The _____ reason for living in this community is that it is so close to campus.

prime, primary, primarily

5. Many students have the _____ that it is cheaper to rent an apartment than to stay in a dormitory.

perceive, perception, perceptive, perceptively

6. I always lock the door _____ when I leave the house.

security, secure, securely

7. I have almost made up my mind which apartment to rent, but I'll _____ my plans next week.

final, finalize, finally

8. There were too many _____ when I lived on campus, so this year I'm looking forward to more freedom living off campus.

restrict, restriction, restrictive

9. The college has plans for the _____ of two new dormitories next year.

construct, construction

10. Although the apartment complex has an _____ appearance on the outside, it is quite modern and comfortable on the inside.

institution, institutionalize, institutional

5. COLLOCATIONS

5A In the space provided, write the word that can precede all four words in each group to form common collocations.

| labor | computer | primary | maintenance | positive |

1. *maintenance*   work, person, equipment, contract

2. _____   color, election, school, function

3. _____   Day, negotiations, of love, union

4. _____   graphics, language, literacy, science

5. _____   statement, result, number, attitude

| residential | prime | security | final | community |

6. _____   guard, blanket, risk, deposit

7. _____   college, spirit, leader, center

8. _____   exam, decision, stage, result

9. _____   care, customers, treatment, community

10. _____   minister, suspect, number, time

5B Complete each sentence with an appropriate collocation from exercise A.

1. I asked the landlord to send the maintenance ____*person*____ to fix my broken window.

2. The hours between 8:00 and 10:00 in the evening are considered the prime _____ for watching television.

3. The outdoor swimming pool in our community always closes on Labor _____.

4. Although Jill is often sick, she maintains a positive _____ about her health situation.

5. When I entered the government building, a security _____ searched my bag.

6. David attended a community _____ for two years before transferring to a four-year college.

7. A cooperative-learning project took the place of a final _____ in my history class.

8. My favorite teacher in primary _____ was Mrs. Jones, who taught me how to read.

9. My parents live in a safe residential _____ outside Baltimore.

10. I'm taking a course in computer _____ next semester because I want to add some artistic design elements to my website.

6. WORD PARTS

6A Chart Completion

In the chart below, the noun suffixes are used to indicate a person's job, interest, or personal characteristic. Add two more words in each category.

COMMON SUFFIXES			
to indicate a person's job, interest, or personal characteristic			
-ian	-er	-or	-ist
librarian	designer	administrator	biologist
mathematician	gardener	advisor	economist
musician	hiker	author	finalist
politician	interpreter	conductor	individualist
technician	lawyer	creator	linguist
vegetarian	researcher	surveyor	theorist

6B Definitions

Match the words in the chart with the following descriptions.

1. _____designer_____ A person who makes plans for clothes, furniture, and so on

2. _____ Someone who translates from one language into another

3. _____ A person who writes books

4. _____ A person or team that has a good chance of winning a contest or an athletic event

5. _____ Someone who deals with numerical variables

6. _____ A person who does not eat meat

7. _____ A person who directs

8. _____ Someone who runs a business or program

9. _____ A person who provides assistance for legal problems

10. _____ A person who does things in his or her own way

11. _____ A person who develops ideas on a subject

7. WRITING

7A Defining a Term

Find an article on the Internet about **one** of the following topics. (Note: Many colleges and universities have websites that address these issues.)

- security deposits
- subletting
- lease agreements
- eviction

Write a short paragraph that defines the topic you chose. Include several appropriate details to make your definition clear.

7B Paragraph Writing

Write a response to **one** of the following topics. Include at least **six to eight vocabulary words** in your paragraph.

1. Choosing an appropriate roommate can be more difficult than it seems. Your best friend might not be the most appropriate roommate. How can you make sure that your experience living with a roommate is a positive one? Have you had any good or bad experiences with roommates? What issues should a person think about when looking for a roommate?

2. What are the disadvantages and advantages of living in a college dorm? Consider such issues as privacy, noise, roommates, bathrooms, cafeteria food, and room design. Should all college students be required to live in a dorm for at least one year? Why or why not? What advice could you give someone who is about to move into a dorm?

8. SPEAKING

8A Partner Activity: Choosing an Apartment

Discuss with a partner the housing options below.

- What type of resident is each housing unit designed for?
- What are the advantages and disadvantages of each housing unit?
- Which one would you select? Give five reasons for your choice.
- Which one would you definitely not want to rent? Why not?

HILLTOP APARTMENTS
555-4141

Newly constructed! Terrific location!

- friendly administration
- furnished units
- 2 or 3 bedrooms
- free utilities
- maintenance service
- computer access
- social activities
- secure environment
- attractively designed rooms
- laundry facilities
- close to campus—everything within walking distance

$620 per month per unit; yearly contracts only

Glen Valley Apartments

Tours available
Move in now!

We offer 3-bedroom apartments with free computer access, free parking and free transportation to campus.

Our on-site fitness center features a hot tub and pool

Plus:
Game room
Volleyball court
24-hour emergency maintenance

A student-friendly environment!

Security deposit required
Rent: $1,200 per month

Tel: 555-8642

8B Partner/Group Activity: Roommate Search

You and a friend have decided to rent an apartment together. However, the apartment has three bedrooms, and you need a third person to share the rent. Discuss with your friend the type of roommate you are looking for. Then design a survey of at least eight questions that you will use to try to find the perfect roommate.

1. _____ *What kinds of food can you cook?* _____

2. _____

3. _____

4. _____

5. _____

6. _____

7. _____

8. _____

9. _____

Using these questions, interview your classmates or friends to try to find the best roommate. Introduce your new roommate to the class and explain why you chose him or her.

For more activities related to this chapter, go to the *Essential Academic Vocabulary* website.

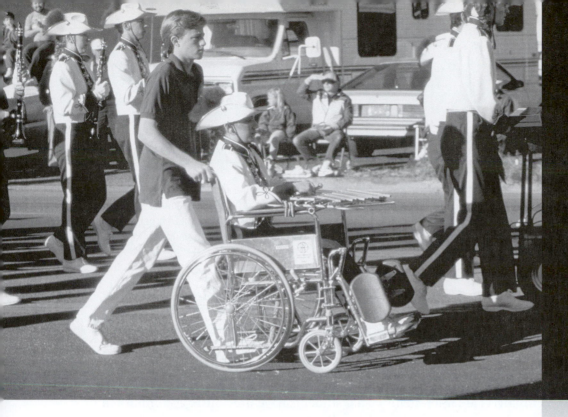

STUDENT ACTIVITIES

WORD LIST

Noun		Verb	Adjective	Adverb
acquisition	focus	affect	cultural	normally
authority	investment	append	random	previously
category	journalist	commission	relevant	traditionally
chapter	lecture	constitute	voluntary	
consequence	legislation	consume		
credit	principle	export		
distinction	region	hurt		
energy	resource	injure		
equation	schedule	participate		
		refine		

PREVIEW QUESTIONS

1. What kinds of extracurricular student activities does your college offer?

2. What extracurricular activities do you participate in?

3. Why did you choose these extracurricular activities?

4. Do you think that your participation in extracurricular activities is important for admission to graduate school or for getting a job? Why or why not?

5. What can you learn from extracurricular activities that you do not learn in the classroom?

6. Do you think that some kinds of extracurricular activities are better than others? For example, is tutoring in an after-school program for children better than playing soccer? Give reasons for your opinion.

READING

EXTRACURRICULAR ACTIVITIES: A MEANS TO AN END

1 Graduate schools and employers are interested in what students have **previously** accomplished in college—beyond attending **lectures**, taking **relevant credit** courses, **consuming** facts and figures, solving mathematical **equations**, and preparing for exams. Successful applications **constitute** more than a high GPA and test scores. However, **appending** extracurricular activities to a résumé

5 will not save students if their grades and scores are too low. Graduate schools and companies need people who can balance their academic **schedules** with their personal lives.

Students' own interests should provide the **focus** for their extracurricular activities. No **category** of activity is better than another. There is no value **distinction** between fraternity **chapters,** literary societies, orchestras, and football teams. However, leadership in one or two

10 activities is often more attractive to admissions **authorities** and employers than **random** membership in many different organizations. Some schools and businesses **traditionally** favor activities that involve **voluntary** service to others (children, the elderly, the sick or **injured,** the homeless), while others may prefer activities that involve the **acquisition** of judgment, efficiency, organization, and cooperation, such as working as a **journalist** for the student newspaper or

15 administering a volunteer project. Students should **normally** focus their **energy** on areas that are of interest to them.

Students in all **regions** have access to a variety of college and community **resources** that **affect** their extracurricular selections. For example, **legislation** has **commissioned** colleges to provide equal sports opportunities and a wider selection of sports to women. As a **consequence,** more

20 women now **participate** in college sports, while some traditionally men's sports have been discontinued.

In **principle,** students should consider experiences that will help them to **refine** their skills outside the classroom as an **investment** in their future with potential positive consequences. Students should consider stepping outside their comfort zones and push themselves to learn

25 about and interact with diverse **cultural** communities. The skills acquired in extracurricular activities can be **exported** to future activities in the workplace.

Adapted from *Extracurricular Options for Pre-meds*, 10/17/03,
http://www.studentaffairs.columbia.edu/preprofessional/health/extra_curricular.php

1. VOCABULARY IN CONTEXT

Find the boldface words in the text that correspond to the following meanings.

Paragraph 1

a. _____ at an earlier time

b. _____ a statement of the equality of two amounts

c. _____ using in large amounts

d. _____ are considered as

Paragraph 2

e. _____ gain

f. _____ type or variety

g. _____ usually

h. _____ difference

i. _____ local division of a larger organization

j. _____ main point

k. _____ people who are hurt

l. _____ existing for a long time

Paragraph 3

m. _____ laws

n. _____ result

o. _____ given official authority

p. _____ influence

Paragraph 4

q. _____ sent out

r. _____ effort and time to get an advantage

s. _____ in general

t. _____ relating to customs and beliefs of a group of people

2. READING COMPREHENSION

2A Getting the Facts

Put a check mark (✓) next to the statements that are **true**, according to the information in the reading.

a. _____   Admission to a graduate school depends only on a student's GPA.

b. _____   Extracurricular activities can compensate for very low grades when applying for graduate school admission or jobs.

c. _____   It is better to be a member of the college orchestra than to be a member of a fraternity.

d. _____   Some graduate schools and employers prefer to admit students with service-oriented activities.

e. _____   Journalism is an example of a service-oriented activity.

f. _____   Students should try to participate in a wide range of activities, even if they are not interested in them.

g. _____   Recent legislation has favored men's sports over women's sports.

h. _____   Students should think of extracurricular activities as a possible advantage to their careers.

i. _____   Staying within one's comfort zone requires little effort.

j. _____   Participating in extracurricular activities wastes too much valuable time.

2B Making Inferences

The following table shows the percentage of students from some different majors who participate in various kinds of extracurricular activities at one particular college. Study the table and draw some inferences from the information provided.

Survey of Participation in Extracurricular Activities				
	Psychology	Education	Engineering	Foreign Languages	Business
Music and Dance Groups	19%	35%	4%	29%	15%
Organizations Related to Academic Major	68%	48%	82%	73%	40%
Fraternity/Sorority	10%	15%	13%	15%	35%
Recreational Sports	51%	24%	41%	49%	30%
Student Government	2%	5%	1%	15%	45%
Minority or International Student Organizations	4%	25%	65%	65%	25%
Religious Groups	3%	29%	14%	36%	8%

1. What can you infer from the percentages for minority and international student organizations at this college?

   _____

   _____

2. What can you infer about student government organizations at this institution?

   _____

   _____

3. How would you describe the average business student?

   _____

   _____

4. Why do you think that the most popular student organizations are related to academics?

_____

_____

5. What surprises you about the information provided in this table?

_____

_____

6. How does the information here relate to your own knowledge about student organizations at your college or university?

_____

_____

> Practice new words in listening, reading, speaking, and writing activities with the goal of achieving fluency in all these skills.

3. DICTIONARY SKILLS

Read the dictionary entries and write a short definition for each phrase below.

> **cul•tur•al** (kŭl′chər əl) *adj.* Relating to culture: *Paris is the cultural center of France. Cultural influences affect individual behavior.* **–cul′tur•al•ly** *adv.*
> **cul•ture** (kŭl′chər) *n.* **1.** [C] The arts, beliefs, customs, institutions, and all other products of human work and thought at a particular time: *the various cultures of Africa.* **2.** [U] The qualities of mind and the tastes that result from appreciation of the arts and sciences: *a writer of great culture.* **3.** [U] The breeding of animals or growing of plants, especially to improve their development: *bee culture.* **4.a.** [U] The growing of microorganisms or tissues under special conditions for scientific study or use in medicines. **b.** [C] Such a growth, as of bacteria or tissue: *a culture of penicillin-producing mold.* **–tr.v.** **cul•tured, cul•tur•ing, cul•tures.** To grow (microorganisms, tissues, or other living matter) for scientific study.
> **cul•tured** (kŭl′chərd) *adj.* **1.** Well educated; having appreciation for the arts: *a cultured supporter of the ballet.* **2.** Grown or produced under artificial and controlled conditions: *cultured pearls.*

1. cultural heritage: *ways of living and thinking that have existed for a long time in a society*

2. cultured pearls: _____

3. culture shock: _____

4. a poet of great culture: _____

5. a lab culture: _____

6. cultural diversity: _____

7. cultural identity: _____

8. popular culture: _____

9. cultural activities: _____

10. a cultured person: _____

4. WORD FORMS

4A Chart Completion

Complete the following chart with the different forms of each word. Note that some words do not have all forms.

Noun	Verb	Adjective	Adverb
	consume		X
	injure		X
category			
	participate		X
legislation, legislator			X
acquisition			X
	export	X	X
	X		traditionally
region			
			normally
resource	X		

4B Word Forms in Sentences

Reread the second and third paragraphs in the reading selection. Complete the following summary with the words in the box. Make sure that each word fits grammatically and meaningfully.

acquire	injuries	participation	tradition
categorized	normally	random	voluntary
energy	participate	regional	

Students' own interests should provide the focus for their (1) _____ in extracurricular activities. Activities are not (2) _____ according to a value judgment. Fraternity chapters, literary societies, orchestras, and football teams are equally considered. However, students who (3) _____ in one or two activities are probably more attractive to admission authorities and employers than students who are involved in a range of (4) _____ organizations. Some schools and businesses have a (5) _____ of favoring (6) _____ service to others (children, the elderly, those with (7) _____, and those with no home), while others may prefer activities that require students to (8) _____ judgment, efficiency, organization, and cooperation, such as being a journalist for the student newspaper or administering a (9) _____ volunteer project. Students should (10) _____ focus their (11) _____ on areas that interest them.

5. COLLOCATIONS

Give **two examples** of things associated with each of the following common collocations.

1. major exports _____ *oil* _____   _____ *rice* _____

2. algebraic equations _____   _____

3. fuel consumption _____   _____

4. voluntary service _____   _____

5. culturally diverse societies _____   _____

6. acquired tastes _____   _____

7. traditional holidays _____   _____

8. refined products _____   _____

9. alternative energy   _____ _____

10. consumer products   _____ _____

11. credit courses   _____ _____

12. sports injuries   _____ _____

13. regional attractions   _____ _____

14. ancient cultures   _____ _____

6. WORD PARTS

port (carry)

6A Each of the words in the box contains the word part *port*, which means "carry." Write each word next to its meaning.

deportation	portable	report
export	porter	reporter
import	portfolio	transportation
port		

1. _____ a product received from another country

2. _____ a person who carries travelers' bags

3. _____ a place where ships are loaded and unloaded

4. _____ a piece of news

5. _____ the act of making a person return to his or her country

6. _____ a system of carrying items from one place to another

7. _____ able to be carried easily

8. _____ an artist's collection of work

9. _____ a product sent to another country

10. _____ a journalist who writes about the news

6B Each of the following words containing the word part *port* has two of the items in the box associated with it. Write the words under the appropriate headings.

baggage	computers	laptop computer	suitcase
Boston	designs	New York	trains
cars	editing	nightly news	visa expiration
CD player	electronics	oil	weather forecast
coffee	immigration violations	paintings	writing

1. report

_____

_____

2. portable

_____

_____

3. portfolio

_____

_____

4. port

_____

_____

5. reporter

_____

_____

6. exports

_____

_____

7. imports

_____

_____

8. transportation

_____

_____

9. deportation

_____

_____

10. porter

_____

_____

7. WRITING

7A Writing a Persuasive Letter

As the leader of a student club (e.g., the intramural soccer club, the international student organization, the jazz music club) at your college, you have been asked to write a letter to new students to persuade them to join your organization. Complete a letter explaining the goals of the club, the activities organized by the club, and the benefits of joining the club. Include details of how to join the club and when and where the first meeting will be held. Try to include at least **six to eight vocabulary words** in your letter. The letter has been started for you.

August 4

Dear New Student:

I wish to welcome you to campus. I expect you have given a lot of thought to the credit courses you are going to take, but perhaps you are still unsure whether to participate in sports, student government, or a volunteer organization. To assist you in making these important decisions, let me tell you more about this organization which has helped me in so many truly relevant ways since my first day on campus three years ago.

_____

_____

_____

_____

_____

_____

_____

_____

_____

_____

_____

_____

_____

_____

7B Paragraph Writing

Write a response to **one** of the following topics. Include at least **six to eight vocabulary words** in your paragraph.

1. What activities did you participate in during high school? Were you interested in music, athletics, volunteer activities, or academic clubs? How do you think these activities have affected your life today? Do you think they helped you make friends or get into college? Are you still interested in the same activities now? Why or why not?

2. Describe your own experiences with extracurricular activities in college. What organizations have you joined? Why did you join them? Describe your own role in the organization as a leader or participant. Comment on whether you think it is difficult to balance activities and studying.

8. SPEAKING

8A Conducting an Interview

You will be interviewing a student about a campus organization that he or she has joined and report the information back to a small group or the class. Prepare for your interview by writing eight questions to ask about the organization (name, activities, meeting times, requirements, etc.).

	Questions	Answers
1.	Have you joined any student organizations? Please name one organization that you have joined.	
2.		
3.		
4.		
5.		
6.		
7.		
8.		

Conduct your interview in a public place, such as a cafeteria, the student center, or the recreation center. Politely ask a student to participate in your survey. Conduct the interview, and record the student's answers in the answers column. Remember to thank the student for his or her cooperation.

Give a short oral report (about three minutes) on the interview to a small group or the class regarding the information you learned about one student organization.

The following expressions are useful in conducting interviews:

Asking for an interview

- Would you mind answering a few questions for my class assignment?
- Could you spare a few minutes to answer some questions about a student organization you have joined?

Asking for more information

- Could you explain what you mean by that?
- Could you be more specific?
- Could you give me an example?

Asking for repetition

- Would you mind repeating that?
- I'm not sure I understand what you mean.
- Could you repeat that point?

Thanking the interviewee

- Thank you so much for your help.
- Thank you for answering my questions today.

8B Role-Plays

Using new vocabulary words from this chapter, act out the following role-plays.

1. At the beginning of the semester, you decided to join the band, the soccer team, the campus events committee, the chess club, and the French club. Initially it was fun, and you have met a lot of new people. However, you are now falling behind in your studies, and you realize that you should eliminate some of these activities. The problem is that you like them all. You decide to discuss this problem with a friend who seems to be better at time management than you are. Your friend advises you about which activities to keep and which ones to drop.

2. In the school newspaper you see an advertisement regarding a meeting for students interested in joining the ski club. A phone number is provided, but there is very little additional information. Call the telephone number and ask the club member for details about the following:

- the date, time, and location of the meetings
- the criteria for joining
- the activities of the club: ski trips and other events
- any special equipment needed
- the cost of membership

For more activities related to this chapter, go to the *Essential Academic Vocabulary* website.

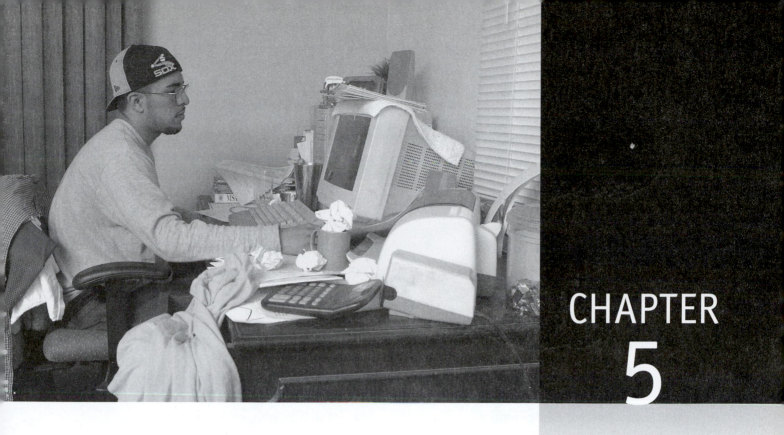

REVIEW

PREVIEW SENTENCES

Examine the photograph of a student sitting at his computer late at night. Put a check mark (✓) next to the statements that might indicate that he has a problem with computer addiction.

Definition: ***Addiction*** *is dependence on a harmful habit, such as alcohol, drugs, or smoking.*

1. _____ George has been sitting at his computer for a short period of time.

2. _____ George likes to work in a comfortable environment.

3. _____ George has designed a new website with several interesting features.

4. _____ George focuses more on playing computer games than on studying.

5. _____ George rarely participates in student activities.

6. _____ George prefers the online community to interacting with other residents in his dorm.

7. _____ George derives pleasure from playing computer games occasionally.

8. _____ George's computer habits have a significant impact on his social life.

9. _____ George normally restricts his computer use to one or two hours per day.

10. _____ George's major is computer science, so most of his assignments are computer based.

11. _____ George uses his computer skills to assist him in his research.

12. _____ Surfing the Internet consumes much of George's spare time.

1. VOCABULARY IN CONTEXT

Write the appropriate word from each group of word choices in the numbered blanks in the text.

1. beneficial, legal, voluntary
2. significant, theoretical, traditional
3. affected, contracted, involved
4. categories, elements, periods
5. chapter, computer, schedule
6. consuming, establishing, occurring
7. achieve, range, select
8. primary, similar, traditional
9. indicates, obtains, surveys
10. focus, investment, potential

11. define, function, refine
12. derive, evaluate, participate
13. design, finalize, perceive
14. distribution, impact, resource
15. creating, legislating, restricting
16. affect, estimate, seek
17. assistance, community, evidence
18. issue, principle, regulation
19. achieve, assess, consult
20. methods, policies, sections

COMPUTER ADDICTION ON CAMPUS

There is no doubt that computers have had (1) _beneficial_ effects on the way we work, study, and play. However, computer addiction has become a (2) _____ problem for some students whose lives are (3) _____ by long (4) _____ of time spent in front of a (5) _____ screen. Instead of (6) _____ face-to-face relationships on campus, these students (7) _____ the computer as their (8) _____ method of interaction. Research (9) _____ that these students have a greater (10) _____ for failing their classes and dropping out of college because they are unable to (11) _____ academically and socially.

It is not always easy for students to (12) _____ whether their computer use has become an addiction or not. However, if they (13) _____ a negative (14) _____ on their grades or if they seem incapable of (15) _____ their own computer use, then it may be time to (16) _____ professional (17) _____ on this (18) _____. A college counselor can (19) _____ the problem and advise students of effective (20) _____ to stop their addiction.

2. SYNONYMS

Match the nouns in column A with their meanings in column B.

Column A	Column B
1. _____ labor	**a.** part of one hundred
2. _____ region	**b.** surroundings
3. _____ percent	**c.** management
4. _____ consequence	**d.** safety
5. _____ environment	**e.** careful examination
6. _____ administration	**f.** mathematical statement
7. _____ regulation	**g.** work
8. _____ legislation	**h.** well-planned action
9. _____ analysis	**i.** proof
10. _____ evidence	**j.** written legal agreement
11. _____ contract	**k.** special attention
12. _____ focus	**l.** area
13. _____ equation	**m.** result
14. _____ security	**n.** rule
15. _____ strategy	**o.** law

3. WORD FORMS

3A Chart Completion

Give the noun form for each of the following verbs.

Verb	Noun	Verb	Noun
identify	*identity*	conduct	
theorize		analyze	
major		create	
formulate		categorize	
assist		select	
survey		maintain	
reside		regulate	
administer		interpret	

3B Word Forms in Sentences

Write the appropriate word from each group of word choices below the reading in the numbered blanks in the text.

1. assist, assistance, assistant
2. community, communication, communion
3. secure, secured, security
4. elementary, elemental, element
5. survey, surveyed, surveyor
6. appropriate, appropriateness, appropriately
7. regulates, regulations, regulatory
8. maintain, maintenance, maintained
9. consequently, consequent, consequence
10. design, designed, designing
11. invest, investment, investor
12. purchase, purchaser, purchased
13. acquire, acquired, acquisition
14. residence, reside, resident
15. commission, commissioned, commissioner

When my family and I arrived in Boston so that I could attend graduate school, I went to the campus housing office to get (1) _____ in finding a place to live. I told the advisor that I wanted to live in a quiet (2) _____. I also wanted to make sure that my children were safe, so (3) _____ was an important (4) _____ in my search. I (5) _____ several properties, but nothing seemed (6) _____. One apartment unit had too many (7) _____, such as not allowing pets. Another had poor (8) _____ and, as a (9) _____, some of the appliances were broken. Another house had an unattractive (10) _____. However, I finally found a suitable house. In fact, the price was right, and it seemed like such a good (11) _____ that I decided to (12) _____ it instead of renting it. This (13) _____ meant that both the seller and I were happy. I found a comfortable (14) _____, and the real estate agent received a good (15) _____ on the sale.

4. COLLOCATIONS

Combine a word from column A with a word from column B to form a common collocation. Then match the two-word collocation with its definition.

Column A	Column B
statistical	attitude
final	exams
financial	conduct
legal	number
yearly	data
disorderly	union
sports	income
prime	section
labor	issue
positive	assistance

1. _____sports section_____ the part of the newspaper devoted to sports

2. _____ aggressive or intoxicated behavior

3. _____ money that is given or loaned

4. _____ salary earned annually

5. _____ a good outlook on life

6. _____ a figure that cannot be divided by another figure

7. _____ an organization for workers

8. _____ tests taken at the end of the semester

9. _____ a problem with the law

10. _____ information from numbers

5. WORD PARTS

Complete each sentence with an appropriate word from the box. Use clues in the sentences as well as your knowledge of the meaning of prefixes, suffixes, and roots to assist you.

administrator	deportation	incomplete	porter	vegetarian
advisor	evidence	nonsmoking	portfolio	visibility
creator	immature	nonstop	revise	vision

1. Tom must _____ his paper before turning it in tomorrow.

2. At the party last Saturday, there was _____ music, and everyone danced all night long.

3. I was asked to bring a _____ of my artwork to show during my interview for a graphic arts job.

4. In my job as a hospital _____, I have to interact with both doctors and patients.

5. Although Mary is almost 30, her behavior is sometimes very _____.

6. The _____ at the crime scene proves that the man with short, dark hair is guilty.

7. There was a terrible accident on the highway today because of poor _____ in the foggy conditions.

8. The _____ of this technology also invented a new kind of transportation system.

9. International visitors can face _____ if they do not obey the conditions of their visa.

10. People normally wear glasses or contact lenses to correct their _____.

11. I received a grade of _____ because I did not finish my research paper on time.

12. My _____ suggested that I take five academic courses next semester.

13. When Dr. Jones arrived at the airport, a _____ assisted her with her luggage.

14. I prefer to eat in the _____ section of a restaurant so that I can breathe more easily.

15. I took my cousin, who is a _____, to a wonderful new café that serves food made from the freshest vegetables and fruit.

Address: http://elt.heinle.com/essentialvocab › go

For more activities related to this chapter, go to the *Essential Academic Vocabulary* website.

EDUCATION

WORD LIST

Noun		Verb	Adjective	Adverb
circumstance	job	alter	considerable	correspondingly
compensation	levy	comment	constant	
component	location	ensure	dominant	
constraint	minority	illustrate	ethnic	
core	outcome	react	initial	
decade	philosophy		intermediate	
diversity	proportion		sufficient	
emphasis	reliance			
framework	sex			
funds	shift			
grade	task			
immigrant	technique			
integration	vision			
interaction				

PREVIEW QUESTIONS

1. What do you notice about the children in the photo-graph? What special challenges might a teacher encounter with students who come from different countries and speak different languages?

2. Why do you think there are so many students from dif-ferent cultures in U.S. schools?

3. Think back to your elementary-school or high-school years. Were those years happy or unhappy? Would you want your children to have the same experience? Explain why or why not.

4. Describe the other students at your college. Do they all come from similar cultural and economic back-grounds? How do the students get along together?

5. Have you ever considered becoming a teacher? Why or why not?

READING

SHIFTING CHALLENGES IN EDUCATION

1   Mrs. Margaret Tanner's classroom in a sunny, southern California elementary school is similar to any other fifth-**grade** room in communities all over the United States. The school was constructed in the 1950s, and the **core** number of students it serves has remained around 600 since its opening. Since she started teaching there in 1981, Mrs. Tanner has had as few as 19

5 students in her classroom and as many as 35, but on the average, her daily attendance is between 26 and 28 students of both **sexes**.

  Mrs. Tanner has taught fifth grade in this classroom, in this school, in a suburb of Los Angeles, for 24 years. At the core of her **philosophy** of education is her **emphasis** on student **interaction** as a **framework** for successful educational **outcomes** for all students. When she

10 accepted her **initial** teaching assignment, the **dominant** student population was middle class, white, and English speaking—the descendents of people who had emigrated to the United States from Europe during the nineteenth and early twentieth centuries. In short, they were very similar to Mrs. Tanner herself.

  In that first **decade** of her professional career, however, demographic **shifts** took place in

15 California. Los Angeles expanded and its suburbs multiplied, and her community became a popular **location** for recently arrived Mexican **immigrants** and other Spanish-speaking people coming to California from towns and cities in the southwestern United States. **Correspondingly,** the **proportions** of white and **minority** children in Mrs. Tanner's fifth-grade class also began to change. Her white, middle-class students were joined by African American children whose

20 parents had relocated from the southern United States and by children who spoke Spanish in their working-class homes and commuted regularly between the United States and Mexico. The parents of these children, like the grandparents of her earlier students, had come to the United States to find employment with **sufficient** financial **compensation** to **ensure** a higher standard of living for their families.

25   Since the second decade of Mrs. Tanner's teaching career, **considerable** shifts in the population have continued to **alter** the demographics of her students. More and more, she is teaching children who speak a variety of languages in their homes and communities, including Spanish, Vietnamese, Russian, Hmong, Chinese, and Farsi. In the classroom, students' English abilities may be at the beginning, **intermediate**, or advanced level. The students come from

30 families who have immigrated to the United States to seek a better standard of living, to find freedom from political or religious **constraints**, or to escape from dangerous **circumstances** in their own countries.

Mrs. Tanner has **reacted** to these demographic changes by remaining **constant** in her enthusiasm and her **vision** for her teaching **job**, but she is also the first to admit that the **ethnic**
35 **diversity** of her students **illustrates** the challenges of her role as a teacher and of her understanding of the **tasks** and **techniques** necessary to teach her students effectively. As she **comments**, her greatest challenge is now the cultural diversity of her students, who come from different countries, language backgrounds, and economic levels. In order to reach her diverse students while creating a positive learning environment, **components** that address the
40 **integration** of cultural and language differences must enter into her teaching strategies. At the same time, the school's **reliance** on state **levies** for **funds** may constrain her efforts to teach the various minority groups in her classroom in the most effective ways.

Note: *Demographics* refers to the characteristics of people who live in a specific area. The word is derived from the Greek words *demo* (people) and *graph* (record or write).

Adapted from Eugene Garcia, *Student Cultural Diversity: Understanding and Meeting the Challenge,* 3rd ed. (Boston: Houghton Mifflin, 2002), 4–5.

1. VOCABULARY IN CONTEXT

Choose the best meaning according to the context in which the word is used in the reading.

a. core (line 3)	apple	attention	<u>heart</u>
b. framework (line 9)	attitude	evidence	structure
c. initial (line 10)	final	first	writing
d. dominant (line 10)	constitutional	major	potential
e. shifts (line 14)	changes	dresses	jobs
f. proportions (line 18)	percentage	relationship	size
g. sufficient (line 23)	available	enough	specific
h. compensation (line 23)	exchange	insurance	salary
i. alter (line 26)	argue	change	repeat
j. constraints (line 31)	behavior	concepts	restrictions
k. tasks (line 36)	assignments	duties	policies
l. techniques (line 36)	design	science	skills
m. comments (line 37)	counts	replies	says
n. components (line 39)	factors	formulas	functions
o. funds (line 41)	data	money	proportions

2. READING COMPREHENSION

2A Getting the Facts

Read the following statements about the reading selection. Identify which statements are true (**T**) and which are false (**F**).

a. _____ Mrs. Tanner has been teaching since the 1950s.

b. _____ Mrs. Tanner teaches sixth-grade students.

c. _____ The average number of students per day in Mrs. Tanner's class is currently 27.

d. _____ Mrs. Tanner has changed teaching jobs several times.

e. _____ Mrs. Tanner is a white, middle-class American.

f. _____ During her first years as a teacher, a minority of her students were white.

g. _____ The students in her class now come from many different countries.

h. _____ Some of Mrs. Tanner's students do not speak English as their first language.

i. _____ Mrs. Tanner's teaching style has not changed during her teaching career.

j. _____ A lack of government money may influence the way Mrs. Tanner responds to the needs of her minority students.

2B Making Inferences

1. The families of Mrs. Tanner's students have come to California from all over the world. Using information from the reading and making inferences from your own general knowledge, complete the chart about each ethnic group.

Ethnic Group or Nationality	Language	Country/Area of Origin
Mexicans	Spanish	Mexico
	Vietnamese	
	Russian	
	Hmong	
	Chinese	
	Farsi	

2. Immigrants to the United States come from many other countries besides those mentioned in the reading. What other ethnic groups have immigrated in large numbers to the United States in recent years and for what reasons?

The best way to remember new words is to associate them with words that you already know.

_____

_____

_____

3. DICTIONARY SKILLS

Match the following common "work" expressions with their meanings.

task (ta˘sk) *n.* **1.** A piece of work assigned or done as part of one's duties: *daily tasks.* **2.** A difficult or tedious undertaking: *the task of building a nation.* ♦ **take to task.** To scold sbdy.: *The teacher took all of us to task for not doing our homework.*

SYNONYMS: task, job, chore, assignment. These nouns mean a piece of work that one must do. **Task** means a well-defined responsibility that is sometimes burdensome and is usually required by sbdy. else: *The receptionist's main task is to answer the telephones.* **Job** often means a specific short-term piece of work: *We spent the day doing odd jobs around the house.* **Chore** often means a minor, routine, or odd job: *I have to finish my chores before I'm allowed to go out.* **Assignment** usually means a task given to one by a person in authority: *For tonight's assignment, read the first chapter.*

task force *n.* A temporary grouping of forces and resources for a specific goal: *a military task force.*

a steady job	job security	workaholic	workout
foreign assignment	odd jobs	working class	workplace
job description	on-the-job training	workload	works of art
job satisfaction	task force		

1. ___*a steady job*___   a permanent job

2. _____   a group of people in a society who usually earn relatively little money in jobs that may involve physical labor

3. _____   the likelihood that a job will last a long time

4. _____   small tasks and repairs that need to be done around the house

5. _____   the place where people perform their jobs

6. _____   a group of people organized for a specific goal

7. _____   getting initial experience while working

8. _____   physical exercise

9. _____ objects such as paintings, drawings, and statues

10. _____ the amount of work to be done in a specific period of time

11. _____ sent to work overseas by one's company

12. _____ a list of responsibilities and tasks for a job

13. _____ the positive feeling of knowing that a job is meaningful

14. _____ a person who is addicted to working all the time

4. WORD FORMS

4A Chart Completion

Complete the following chart with the different forms of each word. Note that some words do not have all forms.

Noun	Verb	Adjective	Adverb
emphasis	emphasize	emphatic	emphatically
	illustrate		X
		sufficient	
interaction			
		dominant	
	alter		
			correspondingly
location		X	X
reaction			X
	comment	X	X
		initial	

4B Word Forms in Sentences

Use the correct word form from the chart in the previous exercise to complete the following sentences. Make sure the word you choose fits meaningfully and grammatically into the sentence.

1. initial   Mrs. Tanner's students were _____*initially*_____ the descendents of immigrants from Europe.

2. interaction   Mrs. Tanner's classes are _____; she expects her students to participate actively with her and with each other.

3. dominant   Over the years, the _____ ethnic groups in California have changed.

4. location   Many immigrants prefer to _____ their businesses in California because they can usually make a good living there.

5. sufficient   Some students do not have _____ English skills to participate equally in the classroom.

6. comment   Parents generally make positive _____ on the quality of education in Mrs. Tanner's class.

7. illustrate   The walls of the classroom were decorated with _____ from magazines and newspapers.

8. emphasis   There is _____ agreement among teachers to utilize tasks and techniques that address the ethnic diversity of their classes.

9. reaction   Many studies have shown that immigrant children _____ well to bilingual education.

10. correspondingly The cost of living in California is high, but the salaries for teachers are _____ higher than in some other states.

5. COLLOCATIONS

The following nouns are commonly found with specific verbs and adjectives.

Verbs	Adjectives	Noun
place, put, give	great, considerable, special, main, unnecessary	**emphasis**
establish, set, provide, create, build	basic, broad, general, theoretical, strong	**framework**
produce, achieve, evaluate, predict	possible, satisfactory, successful, disappointing	**outcome**
obtain, raise, receive, administer, provide	(in)sufficient, public, (un)limited, special	**funds**
perform, complete, carry out, avoid	challenging, routine, administrative, time-consuming, rewarding	**task**

Complete the sentences with an appropriate verb, adjective, or noun from the chart.

1. Teachers place considerable ___*emphasis*___ on successful outcomes for all students.

2. One of the tasks of government is to establish a _____ framework for public education.

3. Schools need to receive _____ funds to operate successfully.

4. School managers carry out _____ tasks such as writing reports and keeping records.

5. Most parents _____ great emphasis on a good education for their children.

6. This course provides a _____ framework for the study of psychology, but the internship will provide practical experience.

7. My chemistry professor predicted a successful _____ for my research project.

8. Some state universities have to increase the cost of tuition because they received insufficient _____ from the state government.

9. I thought that Dr. Niven _____ unnecessary emphasis on the Civil War in the final exam because she had barely mentioned it in class.

10. Before we could plan our field trip, we had to _____ sufficient funds to cover the expenses.

7B Paragraph Writing

Write a response to **one** of the following topics. Include at least **six to eight vocabulary words** in your paragraph.

1. Who was your favorite teacher in elementary school or high school? What do you remember about this teacher? What special personal qualities did this person possess? What made this teacher different from other teachers? What special teaching strategies did this teacher use to motivate students? Can you identify the teacher's philosophy of education?

2. Testing is widely used to evaluate learning in individual classes and to assess students for college admission. Testing methods may include writing an essay, answering multiple-choice questions, or writing short answers. Which kind of test do you prefer? Do you think that these tests accurately assess your strengths and weaknesses? Why or why not? What other methods could be used to evaluate your academic performance?

8. SPEAKING

8A Pair Interviews

Discuss with your partner the following questions about your partner's experience in high school. Write your notes in the space provided.

	Questions	Notes
1.	What do you think are the components of a good education?	
2.	What is your philosophy of education?	
3.	Were sufficient funds available for educational activities in your school?	
4.	What were the core subjects that you had to study in high school?	
5.	What kinds of effective techniques did your teachers use?	

	Questions	Notes
6.	What kind of interaction was expected between students and the teacher?	
7.	What was the proportion of students who went to college in your graduating class?	
8.	Which minority groups were represented in your school?	
9.	What kinds of cultural issues were emphasized in your school?	
10.	What comments do you have about the educational system as a whole?	

Using your notes, orally summarize your partner's ideas and experiences back to your partner. Remember to use as many words as possible from Chapter 6. Your partner should monitor the oral summary carefully for accuracy.

8B Group Discussion: To Be a Teacher . . . or Not

In small groups, discuss and write down the *pros* and *cons* (advantages and disadvantages) of becoming a teacher. Consider such factors as status, compensation, benefits, vacation time, classroom management, student motivation, and school environment. When you have finished, summarize your notes orally to another group or the whole class.

The following polite expressions may be useful in your discussion:

Giving opinions

- I think/believe/feel that . . .
- As far as I'm concerned . . .
- In my opinion . . .

Expressing agreement

- I agree with what you said.
- Right/Exactly/True.
- I think so, too.
- You may be right about that.

Expressing disagreement

- I don't really agree with you on that point.
- That might be true, but . . .
- That's a good point, but in my opinion . . .
- I have to disagree with you about that.

Address: http://elt.heinle.com/essentialvocab   › go

For more activities related to this chapter, go to the *Essential Academic Vocabulary* website.

CHAPTER 7

BUSINESS

WORD LIST

Noun	Verb	Adjective	Adverb	Preposition
commodity	access	annual	approximately	despite
corporation	contribute	domestic	subsequently	
document	coordinate	innovative		
justification	demonstrate	negative		
military	implement			
partnership	impose			
professional	link			
promotion	maximize			
resolve	phase out			
scheme	publish			
series	register			
volume	undergo			
	undertake			

PREVIEW QUESTIONS

1. How would you define the term *business*?

2. What factors are necessary to make a business successful?

3. What might be some advantages and disadvantages of starting your own small business?

4. Have you ever worked for a large company? How do you think it is different from working for a small company?

5. What do you know about Procter & Gamble? What kinds of products does the company sell?

6. What innovative products have you seen advertised recently? What company produces them? Are you interested in buying these products? Why or why not?

READING

PROCTER & GAMBLE: AN OPTIMISTIC SCHEME

1   William Procter owned a candle-making business; James Gamble owned a soap business. When the two young business owners married sisters, their father-in-law convinced them of a **scheme** to **link** their businesses together to form a **partnership**. His **justification** was that a partnership would have a much better chance of surviving the **negative** business environment that small
5   businesses were experiencing in the United States during the 1930s. In fact, the United States was **undergoing** a financial crisis. Banks were closing, and there were deep concerns for the economy throughout the country. **Despite** these problems and with the **resolve** of young **professionals**, they formed a partnership in 1837 and **registered** it as Procter & Gamble (P&G). Then they **undertook** to compete with fourteen other soap and candle-makers in Cincinnati,
10   Ohio.

By 1859, their partnership was one of the largest companies in Cincinnati, with **annual** sales of $1 million and eighty employees. During the Civil War, the **volume** of their business continued to grow because Procter & Gamble won government contracts to supply soap and candles to the **military**. **Subsequently**, soldiers took their P&G products home to their families
15   when the war ended in 1865, which **contributed** to the building of brand recognition. Then in 1879, Procter & Gamble introduced Ivory, the "floating" soap. By 1890, Procter & Gamble had grown into a multimillion-dollar **domestic corporation** selling more than thirty different **commodities**. With the invention of the electric lightbulb, candles were **phased out** in the 1920s, but P&G's research laboratory was **coordinating** the production of one **series** of
20   **innovative** products after another. Then in the 1930s, Procter & Gamble used radio advertising to **access** listeners of radio soap operas and to **maximize** its **promotion** of consumer products.

Today, Procter & Gamble is a global corporation that manufactures and markets more than 300 brands of consumer goods with operations in more than seventy countries. Worldwide sales to over five billion customers totaled **approximately** $38.1 billion for 1999 according to
25   **published** financial **documents**. Its sales **demonstrate** its success in **imposing** a presence of at least one P&G product in every home in America. Open your kitchen cabinets; maybe you will find Crisco or Folgers coffee. Go into your laundry room; there you may see Tide or Bounce.

How about Crest toothpaste or Charmin in your bathroom? It was also Procter & Gamble that introduced Pampers—the disposable diaper! Not bad for a partnership scheme **implemented** by
30 two young men at a time of national economic uncertainty.

Adapted from William M. Pride, Robert J. Hughes, and Jack R. Kapoor, *Business,* 7th ed. (Boston: Houghton Mifflin, 2002), 130.

1. VOCABULARY IN CONTEXT

Determine how the boldface words are used in the reading. Then choose the word or phrase that is closest in meaning.

1. __*a*__ **scheme** (line 2)

   a. plan

   b. evidence

   c. crime

2. _____ **link** (line 3)

   a. create

   b. join

   c. transfer

3. _____ **justification** (line 3)

   a. reason

   b. concept

   c. conclusion

4. _____ **resolve** (line 7)

   a. determination

   b. administration

   c. interpretation

5. _____ **undertook** (line 9)

   a. began

   b. shifted

   c. interacted

6. _____ **domestic** (line 17)

   a. relating to the home

   b. relating to pets

   c. relating to one's own country

7. _____ **phased out** (line 18)

   a. introduced slowly

   b. eliminated gradually

   c. exported

8. _____ **promotion** (line 21)

   a. advertisement

   b. promise

   c. acquisition

9. _____ **approximately** (line 24)

   a. specifically

   b. sufficiently

   c. roughly

10. _____ **documents** (line 25)

   a. resources

   b. chapters

   c. records

2. READING COMPREHENSION

2A Getting the Facts

Read the text carefully and match the following dates with corresponding important developments in Procter & Gamble.

1. ____ early 1830s		a.	Procter & Gamble markets its commodities all over the world.
2. ____ 1837		b.	A soap with special features was introduced.
3. ____ 1859		c.	Candle-making was discontinued.
4. ____ early 1860s		d.	Thirty different items were manufactured by Procter & Gamble.
5. ____ 1865		e.	The P&G brand name was given more recognition.
6. ____ 1879		f.	Procter & Gamble used the radio as a method of advertising.
7. ____ 1890		g.	William Procter and James Gamble married sisters.
8. ____ 1920s		h.	Procter & Gamble provided the military with its products.
9. ____ 1930s		i.	Procter & Gamble was registered as a partnership.
10. ____ early 2000s		j.	The company had yearly sales of $1 million.

2B Making Inferences

1. Why do you think a partnership selling soap and candles was successful? In what ways are soap and candles similar?

   _____

   _____

2. How did Procter & Gamble continue its success after candles were no longer an important commodity?

   _____

   _____

3. What is a soap opera? What can you infer about the origin of this term?

   _____

   _____

4. According to the reading, how popular are P&G products in the United States and in other parts of the world?

   _____

   _____

Well-organized material is easier to learn. Make sure your vocabulary cards or journals are clear and easy to understand.

3. DICTIONARY SKILLS

Study the dictionary entry for *domestic/domesticate/domesticity* and answer the following questions.

> **do•mes•tic** (də mĕs′tĭk) *adj.* **1.** Relating to the family or household: *domestic chores.*
> **2.** Tame or domesticated. Used of animals: *cats and other domestic animals.* **3.** Produced in or
> native to a particular country; not foreign or imported: *domestic cars.* **-do•mes′ti•cal•ly** *adv.*
> **do•mes•ti•cate** (də mĕs′tĭ kāt′) *tr.v.* **do•mes•ti•cat•ed, do•mes•ti•cat•ing, do•mes•ti•**
> **cates.** To train (an animal) to live with or be of use to humans; tame: *Human beings domesti-*
> *cated cattle long ago.* **do•mes′ti•cat′ed** *adj.* **-do•mes′ti•ca′tion** *n.* [U]
> **do•mes•tic•i•ty** (dō′ mĕ stĭs′ĭ tē) *n.* [U] **1.** The quality or condition of being domestic.
> **2.** Home life or pleasure in it: *the comforts of domesticity.*

1. Give some examples of domestic chores that you dislike doing.

   _____

   _____

2. Name some animals that are domesticated.

   _____

   _____

3. Name several domestic products that are currently being imported to the United States.

   _____

   _____

4. Identify the major domestic airlines.

   _____

   _____

5. What are some positive features of domesticity?

   _____

   _____

6. Which domestic appliances do you find most useful?

   _____

   _____

7. What kind of work does a domestic do?

   _____

   _____

8. Describe your favorite domestic car.

_____

_____

9. Briefly explain an important current domestic issue in politics.

_____

_____

10. What domestic products made by Procter & Gamble do you use in your daily life?

_____

_____

4. WORD FORMS

4A Chart Completion

Complete the chart with the corresponding noun or verb forms.

Noun	Verb
coordination, coordinator	coordinate
	demonstrate
justification	
	register
resolve, resolution	
	publish
promotion	
	implement
document, documentation	
	domesticate

4B Word Forms in Sentences

Create **five** new sentences about business, using a noun and a verb from the chart in the previous exercise in each sentence.

1. _____ *Financial <u>documents</u> of major corporations are <u>published</u> annually.* _____

_____

2. _____

_____

3. _____

_____

4. _____

_____

5. _____

_____

6. _____

_____

5. COLLOCATIONS

5A The following nouns are typically found in combination with specific verbs. Match the nouns with the verbs to make meaningful phrases.

laws	production	products	regulations	sales	taxes
promote	*sales*	impose	_____		
	_____		_____		
	_____		_____		

arguments	difficulties	events	organizations	problems	programs
resolve	_____	coordinate	_____		
	_____		_____		
	_____		_____		

5B Match the situations in the following sentences with the collocations that describe them.

annual meeting	professional misconduct
antiwar demonstration	promotion prospects
corporate image	recent undertaking
legal documents	registered mail
multinational corporation	television series

1. _____ Lawyers should be involved in creating business partnerships.

2. _____ Procter & Gamble has a reputation for regularly increasing the salaries and responsibilities of its employees.

3. _____ Companies usually send important documents by a special postal service to ensure that they are not lost.

4. _____ All companies are concerned about public perception.

5. _____ Protestors against government military policies marched in Washington, D.C.

6. _____ There have been several recent cases of top executives being accused of criminal mismanagement.

7. _____ The board of directors discussed the activities of the past year and elected new officers.

8. _____ Although the company headquarters is in New York, there are branch offices all over the world.

9. _____ The manager informed the employees about the new product line.

10. _____ Students can learn a lot about business by watching the program about global trade on Tuesday nights.

6. WORD PARTS

multi- (much, many)

6A Match the words that contain the word part *multi-* with their meanings.

1. ____ **multi**lingual		**a.**	using sound, music, and words on computers
2. ____ **multi**media		**b.**	with many colors
3. ____ **multi**millionaire		**c.**	able to speak three or more languages
4. ____ **multi**colored		**d.**	having many parts or sides
5. ____ **multi**cultural		**e.**	involving different academic subjects in one activity
6. ____ **multi**disciplinary		**f.**	relating to groups with a variety of different beliefs and customs
7. ____ **multi**faceted			
8. ____ **multi**ple choice		**g.**	a person whose wealth is several million dollars
9. ____ **multi**purpose		**h.**	able to be used in a variety of ways
10. ____ **multi**tasking		**i.**	ability to do several things at the same time
		j.	offering a choice of answers, but only one is correct

6B Write a synonym or phrase to explain the meaning of the boldface words. Use context clues to help you.

1. My office tasks have **multiplied** since I was promoted to a managerial position, so I have to work longer hours to get them all done.

   _____

   _____

2. The new **multistory** parking garage has sufficient space for all the employees to park their cars.

   _____

   _____

3. The variety of international food stores in this area reflects the **multiethnic** nature of the residents.

   _____

   _____

4. In recent years **multiple births** have become more common for women who undergo special fertility treatments to have children.

    _____

    _____

5. The **multiplex** in the new shopping center is showing so many different movies that we can always find one that we want to see.

    _____

    _____

6C Discuss the following questions with a partner.

1. What are the advantages of being **multilingual**?
2. What are some examples of **multitasking** in today's offices?
3. What kinds of **multidisciplinary** courses might be useful for a student studying for a business degree?
4. What tools or equipment can be considered to be **multipurpose**?
5. What is your favorite type of **multimedia**?

7. WRITING

7A Writing a Summary

See *Appendix IV* for additional information on summarizing.

Reread the article "Procter & Gamble: An Optimistic Scheme." Take notes in your own words about the main ideas in the text. Use your notes to summarize the reading. Include and underline at least **six to eight vocabulary words** in your summary.

7B Paragraph Writing

Write a response to **one** of the following topics. Include at least **six to eight vocabulary words** in your paragraph.

1. The following principles are listed on the Procter & Gamble website. These principles indicate the philosophy of the company toward its labor force and its customers. Write a paragraph explaining what is meant by these principles, giving examples of what you think each one means.

   - We Show Respect for All Individuals
   - The Interests of the Company and the Individual Are Inseparable
   - We Are Strategically Focused in Our Work
   - Innovation Is the Cornerstone of Our Success
   - We Are Externally Focused
   - We Value Personal Mastery
   - We Seek to Be the Best
   - Mutual Interdependency Is a Way of Life

   _____

   http://www.pg.com/company/who_we_are

2. Write a paragraph about a personal experience in the workplace. This experience could range from an after-school job in a fast-food restaurant to a well-paid professional position. Describe the different tasks you had to perform in your job, the positive and negative aspects of the position, and the approximate period of time that you were employed there.

8. SPEAKING

8A Group Presentations: Researching Procter & Gamble

Each member of the group should research one aspect of Procter & Gamble by consulting the company website at http://www.pg.com. Possible topics are as follows:

- products
- P&G history
- careers
- worldwide operations

- awards

- purpose, values, and principles

Each member should give a short oral presentation on the chosen topic to the other members of the group, summarizing the main points. Using the information provided by these reports, the group members should state whether they would be interested in working for Procter & Gamble, addressing such issues as location, job description, career prospects, and company values.

Alternatively, you may choose another company that is well known to members of your group and follow the same format for your research and presentation.

8B Role-Plays

Using new vocabulary words from this chapter, act out the following role-plays.

1. You have an interview for a managerial job at Procter & Gamble. You have prepared for the interview by checking out P&G's website, and you have many questions to ask the interviewer about the philosophy of the company, promotion prospects, overseas assignments, annual salary ranges, professional responsibilities, and company benefits. Role-play the interview, trying to find out as much specific information as possible from the P&G interviewer.

2. You have recently accepted a new job in a multinational corporation that has a strict dress code. You have to buy some new clothes to fit the image of your new job, but you are uncertain what kinds of items to purchase. You are also considering getting a new professional-looking hairstyle. Ask your best friend for advice about the style and color of the clothes you should buy and what type of hairstyle might be appropriate for you.

Address: http://elt.heinle.com/essentialvocab › go

For more activities related to this chapter, go to the *Essential Academic Vocabulary* website.

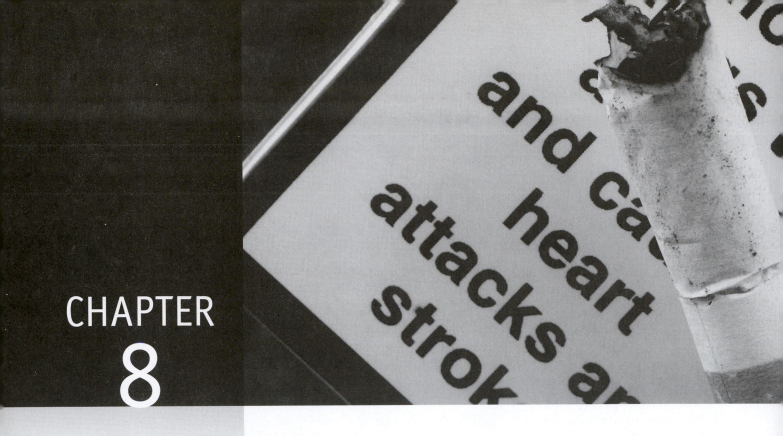

CHAPTER 8

MARKETING

WORD LIST

Noun	Verb	Adjective	Adverb	Conjunction
code	attribute	adult	hence	plus
contrast	communicate	apparent		
cycle	concentrate	ethical		
emergence	exclude	global		
goal	imply	internal		
instance	project	overall		
label	specify	physical		
media (pl.)	target	principal		
objective				
output				
removal				
statistics				
status				
technology				

PREVIEW QUESTIONS

1. What are the effects of advertising on your buying habits? Do you sometimes buy products because you have seen them advertised? What kinds of products might you buy as a result of advertising?

2. What age group do you think is most influenced by advertisements?

3. Which medium do you think is the most effective for advertising: television, radio, newspapers, magazines, the Internet, or billboards? Give reasons for your opinion.

4. Are there some products that should not be promoted through advertisements—for instance, alcohol, cigarettes, unhealthy food items, or personal hygiene items? Why do you think so?

5. Do you believe that cigarette advertisements are responsible for increasing the number of people who smoke? Are the addiction to smoking and any subsequent health problems the responsibility of the individual or the manufacturer?

6. Why do you think cigarettes continue to be advertised despite current knowledge about their unhealthy effects?

READING

MARKETING TOBACCO PRODUCTS AROUND THE WORLD

1 Should tobacco manufacturers be allowed to market their products around the world? Slow growth **plus** legal and regulatory **fights** have made the domestic market less profitable in recent years. **Hence** the search by tobacco companies for more profitable opportunities by **targeting** overseas markets to meet their short-term **objectives** and long-term **goals**.

5 Philip Morris, which markets Marlboro, holds 17 percent of the world cigarette market. British American Tobacco, which markets Lucky Strike, holds 16 percent of the world cigarette market. Winston's maker, R.J. Reynolds, is also a **principal** player in the **output** of tobacco on **global** markets. Japan and Europe are the largest international markets for U.S. tobacco products, although developing countries, where Western brands have particular **status**, are also

10 being targeted. In Malaysia and the Philippines, for **instance**, television ads **project** the joys of smoking American-made cigarettes. In China, where billboards featuring cigarettes are everywhere, consumption is double what it was a few years ago.

Critics charge that the tobacco makers are imposing new **technology** and unethical advertising on consumers to make an unhealthy product attractive. Despite the fact that

15 tobacco product–manufacturers are **excluded** from **communicating** their message on television commercials in the United States and Europe, they face fewer **media** advertising restrictions in many developing countries. The tobacco companies argue that their products are entirely legal and that they use advertising to encourage **adult** smokers to change brand **labels**, not to attract new or underage smokers. However, the **overall statistics** in some developing countries **imply**

20 that the **cycle** of smoking is increasing, with the **emergence** of added **physical** problems **attributed** to this habit.

Clearly, the tobacco companies face more legal pressure in the United States than overseas. Some tobacco manufacturers have been successfully sued under **internal** product-liability laws. In **contrast**, few product-liability cases are filed in Japan or Europe where the **codes** of law tend to

25   favor corporations. This concerns experts, who fear that consumers in other countries have little **apparent** legal recourse against unhealthy products such as cigarettes.

    Specifying the health dangers of smoking, the World Health Organization has called for the global **removal** of tobacco advertising and international controls on tobacco. Meanwhile, the tobacco makers continue to **concentrate** their efforts on international markets. Thus, the **ethical**

30   issue remains: Should cigarette makers be allowed to target global markets?

Adapted from William M. Pride, Robert J. Hughes, and Jack R. Kapoor, *Business,* 7th ed. (Boston: Houghton Mifflin, 2002), 361.

1. VOCABULARY IN CONTEXT

Determine how the words in column A are used in the reading. Then choose the word in column B that is closest in meaning.

Column A	Column B
1. _____ hence (line 3)	a. example
2. _____ goals (line 4)	b. data
3. _____ global (line 8)	c. appearance
4. _____ instance (line 10)	d. direct
5. _____ excluded (line 15)	e. health
6. _____ statistics (line 19)	f. therefore
7. _____ imply (line 19)	g. domestic
8. _____ emergence (line 20)	h. purposes
9. _____ physical (line 20)	i. worldwide
10. _____ attributed to (line 21)	j. elimination
11. _____ internal (line 23)	k. prevented
12. _____ codes (line 24)	l. moral
13. _____ removal (line 28)	m. suggest
14. _____ concentrate (line 29)	n. rules
15. _____ ethical (line 29)	o. resulting from

2. READING COMPREHENSION

2A Getting the Facts

Complete the sentences to make statements that reflect the content of the text. Use the words and phrases in the box.

China	Lucky Strike	the U.S. market
European and Japanese laws	Malaysia	the World Health Organization
international markets	Phillip Morris	U.S. and European laws
Japan		

1. *The World Health Organization* promotes international restrictions on tobacco advertising.

2. _____ controls 17 percent of the global market in cigarettes.

3. _____ has experienced reduced profits because of legal issues and a smaller number of smokers.

4. _____ tend to be on the side of businesses.

5. _____ prohibits direct tobacco advertising on television.

6. _____ is one of the countries with the biggest markets for tobacco products from the United States.

7. _____ allows television ads that promote the status attached to smoking U.S. brands of cigarettes.

8. _____ provide greater opportunities for tobacco manufacturers to make profits.

9. _____ has experienced a doubling of the number of cigarette smokers in recent years.

10. _____ is marketed by a British American company.

2B Making Inferences

1. What could be the legal and regulatory fights that are mentioned in line 2 of the text?

   _____

   _____

2. Why are Western brands of cigarettes considered status symbols? (line 9)

   _____

   _____

3. What type of physical problems might be emerging in developing countries because of the increase in smoking? (line 20)

   _____

   _____

4. Explain what is meant by a *product-liability law*. (line 23)

   _____

   _____

5. What kinds of regulations could the World Health Organization promote to reduce the health dangers of smoking? (line 27)

   _____

   _____

> To avoid becoming confused, do not try to learn similar words at the same time.

3. DICTIONARY SKILLS

Study the dictionary entry for the different forms and meanings of *concentrate* and use the information to complete the following sentences. You may need to change the form or tense of the verb. Include a preposition if necessary.

> **con•cen•trate** (kŏn′sən trāt′) *v.* **con•cen•trat•ed, con•cen•trat•ing, con•cen•trates.** *-intr.* **1.** To keep or direct one's thoughts, attention, or efforts: *It's hard to concentrate on writing a letter with the TV on.* **2.** To come toward or meet in a common center: *The migrating geese concentrate at ponds and streams. -tr.* **1.** To draw or gather (sthg.) toward one place or point; focus: *For centuries the population of Europe has been concentrated in large cities.* **2.** To make (a solution or mixture) stronger. *-n.* [C; U] Something that has been concentrated; *orange juice concentrate.*
> **con•cen•tra•tion** (kŏn′ sən **trā**′shən) *n.* **1.** [U] The act of concentrating; giving close undivided attention: *The secret of doing your work in less time is complete concentration.* **2.** [C] A close gathering or dense grouping: *Lights shone brightly from the concentration of houses in the new development.* **3.** [C] The amount of a particular substance in a given amount of a mixture: *the concentration of salt in seawater.*

1. The marketing efforts of cigarette companies are currently _____ developing countries.

2. My _____ this television program is not very good because advertisements keep interrupting the show.

3. Roadside advertisements tend to be _____ urban areas.

4. Some students can _____ studying even with the TV on.

5. You can figure out how to answer this question if you really _____.

6. This advertisement for lemon _____ is very effective.

7. You will only be successful if you make a _____ effort.

8. According to the advertisement, the _____ of minerals in this bottle of mineral water is quite high.

9. There is a _____ of marketing companies in New York.

10. Right now I'm _____ getting a better score on my final exam in marketing.

4. WORD FORMS

4A Write the appropriate word form from each group in the numbered blanks in the text.

1. emerge, emergence, emerging
2. apparent, apparently
3. global, globalization, globally, globe
4. concentrate, concentrated, concentration
5. implication, imply, implicit
6. communicate, communicates, communications, communicative
7. statistical, statistically, statistics
8. removal, remove, removed
9. specific, specifically, specifics, specify
10. impose, imposed, imposing, imposition

TOBACCO COMPANIES TARGET TRADITIONAL WOMEN

In the 1970s, tobacco companies successfully marketed smoking to women by linking their ad campaigns to the (1) _____women's liberation movement. Now, they are (2) _____ using similar tactics to entice women in traditional societies (3) _____ to take up smoking, *Women's News* reported August 19.

As smoking in the developed world declines, tobacco companies are starting to (4) _____ on new markets in developing nations, especially in Asia. Female smoking rates in these countries have been low historically, a fact that marketers want to change with ads that (5) _____ that smoking (6) _____ equality, fitness, and trendiness. In South Africa, for instance, one ad shows a blonde woman smoking, with the message, "Do I look like I would cook you breakfast?"

As a result, (7) _____ show that female smoking is up in many Third World nations, including Cambodia, Malaysia, and Bangladesh. "Cultural prohibitions against tobacco use by women can be (8) _____ by social change and aggressive tobacco marketing," according to a recent World Health Organization report.

An American Cancer Society report said that tobacco firms are creating cigarette brands (9) _____ for women and sponsoring events such as concerts, art shows, and beauty pageants to appeal to girls. "It goes in waves around the world," said Dr. Omar Shafey, one of the report's editors. "As women experience democratization, they face these pressures intentionally (10) _____ upon them by the tobacco industry. In Lebanon, Egypt, and many [Persian] Gulf countries, women face these pressures."

"To enter the man's world that's taboo is part of the attraction," he added. "As waves of modernization spread, women seek to take up the bad habits of men."

Adapted from Join Together Online, August 28, 2003, http://www.jointogether.org/sa/news/summaries/reader/0,1854,566401,00.html

4B Write **five** statements in your own words about the content of "Tobacco Companies Target Traditional Women." Use one or two of the following words in each statement.

ethical	imply	overall	principal	status
goal	objective	physical	statistics	target

1.   _The apparent goal of tobacco companies is to target women in developing countries._
 _____

2.   _____
 _____

3.   _____
 _____

4.   _____
 _____

5.   _____
 _____

6.   _____
 _____

5. COLLOCATIONS

5A In the space provided, write the word that can precede all four words in each group to form common collocations.

ethical	global	media	physical	statistical

1.   _physical_   exercise, attraction, therapy, education
2.   _____   business, warming, population, travel
3.   _____   event, hype, attention, coverage
4.   _____   analysis, data, information, evidence
5.   _____   behavior, standards, conduct, values

adult	instant	internal	principal	technological

6. _____ medicine, politics, issues, memo

7. _____ problems, solutions, innovations, progress

8. _____ reason, character, method, idea

9. _____ coffee, success, response, access

10. _____ population, language, theme, education

5B Complete each sentence with an appropriate collocation from the previous exercise.

1. The global _population_ has become a target of the tobacco industry.

2. The employees were reminded in an internal _____ that they were not allowed to smoke inside the building.

3. Companies are expected to follow ethical _____ when conducting business.

4. The principal _____ in the movie was played by a popular Hollywood actor.

5. After I hurt my back, I had to have physical _____ for several weeks.

6. The space program has been troubled with numerous _____ problems in recent years.

7. The new CD released by my favorite singer was an instant _____.

8. It is clear from the _____ data in numerous research studies that smoking causes lung disease.

9. The wedding of the famous couple attracted a great deal of _____ coverage.

10. Children cannot go to see movies with an adult _____.

6. WORD PARTS

-ology (the study of . . .)

6A Each of the following words contains the word part *-ology*, which means "the study of. . . ." This word part is very common in the names of academic studies. The job title of the person who works in one of these fields ends in *-ist*: for example, *biologist, archeologist,* and *cardiologist.* The following statements might be made by students taking the courses that follow. Match the appropriate field of study with the statement.

anthropology	biology	meteorology	psychology
archaeology	cardiology	pharmacology	technology
bacteriology	geology		

1. _meteorology_   Today we studied the causes of tornadoes and hurricanes.

2. _____   Next spring our class is going to Egypt to help in the excavation of a newly discovered tomb.

3. _____   This week our professor is discussing the causes of depression.

4. _____   We have just finished studying the layers of rock in the Grand Canyon.

5. _____   As part of our medical training, we will study heart disease.

6. _____   In the lab we often have to use microscopes to study the tiny organisms that cause disease.

7. _____   Tomorrow I have a final exam on the human digestive system.

8. _____   We have to learn all the side effects of common painkillers, such as aspirin and ibuprofen, by the next class.

9. _____   Several professors in our department are well known for their contributions to the telecommunications industry.

10. _____   It is fascinating learning about tribes in the Amazon region who still live hidden from modern life.

6B Which word in the following groups does not have an obvious connection to the other two words? Explain why this word does not relate to the others.

1. biologist, bacteriologist, meteorologist

_____

2. archaeology, criminology, anthropology

_____

3. neurologist, zoologist, ornithologist

_____

4. meteorology, theology, climatology

_____

5. cardiologist, neurologist, geologist

_____

7. WRITING

7A Defining a Term

- A *marketing strategy* is a plan that will enable an organization to make the best use of its resources and advantages to meet its short-term objectives and long-term goals. A marketing strategy consists of (1) the selection and analysis of a *target market* and (2) the creation and maintenance of an appropriate *marketing mix*.
- A *target market* is a group of individuals and/or organizations for which a company develops and maintains a marketing mix suitable for the specific criteria of that group in a manner consistent with the company's overall objectives, after an analysis of the existing competition.
- A *marketing mix* is a combination of product, price, distribution, and promotion developed to satisfy a specific target market.

Adapted from William M. Pride, Robert J. Hughes, and Jack R. Kapoor, *Business,* 7th ed. (Boston: Houghton Mifflin, 2002), 360.

These definitions are marketing terms that may be applied to the selling of any product. For each term, write several sentences related to the marketing of tobacco products to developing countries. Include specific details or examples for each term. The first one is started for you.

1. Marketing strategy: *Because of decreased profits in the domestic market, the marketing strategy of some major tobacco companies is now concentrated on selling cigarettes in developing countries where the profits are likely to increase enormously over the long term. For instance,* _____

2. Target market: _____

_____

_____

_____

_____

_____

_____

3. Marketing: _____

_____

_____

_____

_____

_____

_____

7B Paragraph Writing

Respond to **one** of the following topics with your own opinion. Include at least **eight vocabulary words** in your paragraph.

1. Tobacco companies in the United States are not allowed to advertise their products on television and cannot sell them to minors. Do you think tobacco manufacturers in the United States should be required to follow U.S. laws and regulations when they market their products to other countries?

2. Tobacco companies are not allowed to advertise their products in the United States because cigarettes and other tobacco products are unhealthy and cause illness and death. However, there are many other products, such as fast food and snacks, that are also unhealthy but are legally advertised. Explain your position on the advertising of unhealthy products.

8. SPEAKING

8A Partner Discussion: World Health Organization Facts

Discuss with a partner your reaction to the information in the graphic from the World Health Organization. Consider the following questions:

- How does the World Health Organization try to make an impact with this information?

- Do you think the number of smokers will increase or decrease in the short term? In the long term?

- Why do you think people continue smoking even when they are aware of its potential health problems?

- How does smoking kill people?

- Do warnings on cigarette packages have any effect on smokers' habits?

World Health Organization, November 21, 2003, http://www.cnn.com/HEALTH/9704/16/tobacco.world/

8B Partner Discussion: Analyzing a Cigarette Advertisement

Study the advertisement for cigarettes and analyze the marketing strategy being used to promote this product to the target market. Discuss the following with your partner:

- Demographic targets: age, gender, race, ethnicity, income, education, job, family relationships, religion, and social class

- Psychological targets: personality, motivation, and lifestyle

- Geographic targets: region or state, city size, city image, and urban versus rural

- Behavioral targets: volume of use, benefit expectations, brand loyalty, and price

How do you rate the overall effectiveness of this advertisement?

For more activities related to this chapter, go to the *Essential Academic Vocabulary* website.

ECONOMICS

WORD LIST

Noun	Verb	Adjective	Adverb	Conjunction
attitude	decline	adequate	precisely	whereas
behalf	generate	chemical	temporarily	
challenge	grant	obvious		
commitment	hypothesize	occupational		
compound	monitor	prior		
convention	predict	symbolic		
currency	retain	valid		
dimension				
entity				
image				
investigation				
mechanism				
option				
parameter				
regime				
revenue				

PREVIEW QUESTIONS

1. What necessities of life are free or almost free? Why are they easily available?

2. Name several things that are scarce. How does scarcity affect the price of these items?

3. How do you feel about diamonds? How much do they typically cost?

4. What are some of the traditional occasions for giving diamond jewelry? How did these traditions begin?

5. Where do diamonds come from? What do you know about the methods used to mine and sell diamonds?

6. Explain your reaction to these common sayings about diamonds:

   - "Diamonds are a girl's best friend."

   - "Diamonds are forever."

READING

THE ECONOMICS OF DIAMONDS AND WATER

1   For over 200 years, economists have **hypothesized** about why diamonds are so expensive and water so inexpensive, **whereas** water is so much more useful and necessary. The answer is that relative to the available quantities, more diamonds are wanted than water.

Of course, water is far from free these days. Some people regularly spend over $6 a gallon on
5   bottled drinking water, and most homeowners must pay their local government for tap water. Even air is not always cheap or free. In Mexico City, for example, an **adequate** supply of breathable air is far from free. In this city of 19 million people and 3 million cars, dust, lead, and other **chemical compounds** make the air unsafe to breathe more than 300 days a year. Private companies are now operating oxygen booths in local parks and malls. Breathable air, which costs
10   more than $1.60 per minute, has become a scarce commodity and **generates** considerable **revenue**.

Interestingly, though, diamonds are not all that scarce. The volume of diamonds available for sale has been tightly and carefully **monitored** and controlled. For about 100 years, there has been **precisely** one source for diamonds, De Beers, a South African company, which sells its own
15   diamonds and those from other sources through a single agency, the Central Selling Organization.

The Central Selling Organization has operated a central marketing system on **behalf** of the world's big producers, such as Botswana, Namibia, and Russia and for De Beers' own mines in South Africa. The Central Selling Organization manages the stock of diamonds so that prices do
20   not **decline**. During bad times, the organization collects and stores diamonds **temporarily** until times improve. Then, during good times, the organization releases diamonds to the market in a precisely controlled stream.

Many people argue that De Beers is a monopolist—the only seller—and should, therefore, not be **granted** the ability to **retain** this position in the diamond business. In the United States,
25   monopolies are illegal unless specifically created by the government. In most developed countries, monopolies are either illegal or have strict **parameters** inside which they must operate. De Beers is very careful not to have any **currency** deposited with banks in the United States because of the fear of **investigation** under U.S. law. However, the **attitudes** of other countries,

such as Britain, indicate that a monopoly may be considered a **valid mechanism** of commerce in
some instances. Since diamonds are not used for anything important, it does not particularly
matter if a monopoly exists.

Although diamonds are not particularly useful, the **dimensions** of their attraction to people
are recognized through their beauty and through their power as an **obvious image** of wealth,
success, and love. A U.S. advertising agency invented the slogan "A Diamond Is Forever" for De
Beers **prior** to 1950. De Beers spends about $200 million a year promoting diamonds as a
convention of love. Japanese couples once drank cups of tea when they became engaged to be
married. Instead, De Beers introduced many of them to the **option** of giving diamond
engagement rings as a **symbolic commitment** to marriage. Japan is now the second largest
market for diamonds, after the United States.

A **challenge** to the De Beers' **regime** is **predicted**, as two big newcomers begin mining
diamonds in Canada and Australia. These two major mining **entities** plan to sell outside of the
Central Selling Organization, committing themselves to dealing with the **occupational** stresses of
open-market forces.

Adapted from William Boyes and Michael Melvin, *Fundamentals of Economics,* 2nd ed. (Boston: Houghton Mifflin, 2003), 3–4.

1. VOCABULARY IN CONTEXT

Find the boldface words in the text that correspond to the following meanings.

Paragraphs 1+2

a. _____ income

b. _____ provided a possible explanation

c. _____ combination of two or more elements

d. _____ while on the contrary

Paragraphs 3+4

e. _____ exactly

f. _____ become lower

Paragraph 5

g. _____ keep

h. _____ points of view

i. _____ examination

j. _____ fixed limits

k. _____ reasonable

Paragraphs 6+7

l. _____ before

m. _____ size

n. _____ choice

o. _____ clear

p. _____ relating to a job

q. _____ independent organizations

r. _____ powerful business

s. _____ accepted behavior

t. _____ mental picture

2. READING COMPREHENSION

2A Getting the Facts

Put a check mark (✓) next to the statements that are true, according to the information in the reading.

a. _____ Economics is the study of the production, distribution, and consumption of goods and services.

b. _____ Tap water is free.

c. _____ Air pollution in Mexico City is a health problem.

d. _____ The Central Selling Organization is currently the only agency in the world that sells diamonds.

e. _____ A monopoly is a business that has complete control of a specific market.

f. _____ Private monopolies are legal in the United States.

g. _____ Britain has relaxed attitudes toward monopolies.

h. _____ De Beers diamond advertisements target couples who intend to get married.

i. _____ The Japanese buy more diamonds than Americans.

j. _____ In the future, two new mining companies may change the way that diamonds have traditionally been sold.

2B Making Inferences

1. What are monopolies and why are they illegal in many countries?

   _____

2. According to the reading, the major producers of diamonds are Botswana, Namibia, South Africa, and Russia. Other countries that have diamond mines include Angola, the Democratic Republic of Congo, Canada, and Australia. The countries where diamonds are sold in large numbers are the United States, Britain, and Japan. From this information, write **five** sentences inferring differences between the countries where diamonds are mined and the countries where diamonds are primarily sold.

   a. _The diamond-producing countries are generally poor countries._

   b. _____

   c. _____

   d. _____

   e. _____

   f. _____

> You can learn a large number of words quickly by memorizing the word and its most common meaning. However, in-depth knowledge of a word requires more time and effort.

3. DICTIONARY SKILLS

Study the dictionary entries for the various meanings of *commit* (v.) and *commitment* (n.). Match the following causes with their results.

> **com•mit** (kə mĭt′) *tr.v.* **com•mit•ted, com•mit•ting, com•mits. 1.** To do, perform, or be guilty of (a mistake or crime): *commit a crime; commit a serious blunder.* **2.** [*to*] To place (sbdy./sthg.) in the keeping of another; entrust: *commit oneself to the care of a doctor; commit responsibilities to an assistant.* **3.** To place (sbdy.) in confinement or custody by an official act: *The judge committed the criminal to prison for two years.* **4.** [*to*] To place (sthg.) for future use or preservation: *The spy committed the secret code to memory.* **5.** To promise or obligate (oneself): *He committed himself to finish the project by Friday.*
>
> **com•mit•ment** (kə mĭt′mənt) *n.* **1.** [U] The act of committing: *the commitment of poems to memory.* **2.** [C; U] A promise or an obligation to keep certain beliefs or to follow a certain course of action: *The President takes an oath that is a binding commitment to uphold the laws of the United States.* **3.** [C] The state of being emotionally or mentally bound to another person or to a course of action: *a strong commitment to each other; a deep commitment to help clean up the environment.*

If you . . .
Cause

A likely result is that you will . . .
Result

1. _____ commit a crime
2. _____ have a religious commitment
3. _____ demonstrate commitment to your country
4. _____ commit a serious error at work
5. _____ demonstrate professional commitment
6. _____ commit yourself to a doctor's care
7. _____ meet your financial commitments
8. _____ commit responsibilities to a new employee
9. _____ have a strong emotional commitment
10. _____ are committed to prison
11. _____ have a deep commitment to animal rights
12. _____ commit facts to memory
13. _____ display a lack of political commitment
14. _____ have a social commitment
15. _____ show a lack of commitment to your spouse

a. have more time to work on other projects
b. pay your household bills on time
c. get married
d. volunteer at the animal shelter
e. get fired
f. recover from an illness
g. get caught by the police
h. get divorced
i. work late at the office
j. go to a party
k. attend a church regularly
l. perform well on a test
m. join the army
n. lose your freedom
o. forget to vote in elections

4. WORD FORMS

4A Chart Completion

Complete the following chart with the different forms of each word. Note that some words do not have all forms.

Noun	Verb	Adjective	Adverb
precision	X	*precise*	precisely
		valid	X
investigation, investigator			X
	hypothesize		
		occupational	X
convention			
option			X
	generate		X
	X	adequate	
	retain		X
		symbolic, symbolical	

4B Word Forms in Sentences

Reread "The Economics of Diamonds and Water." Complete the summary of the reading with the following words. Make sure that each word fits grammatically and meaningfully.

challenge	image	monopoly	regime
commitment	investigation	parameters	whereas
decline	monitored	precisely	

For the last 200 years, the buying and selling of diamonds has been carefully (1) _____ by the Central Selling Organization, which manages the supply of diamonds so (2) _____ that prices rarely (3) _____. De Beers, a South African company, has a (4) _____ on the diamond trade that is operated by the Central Selling Organization. However, monopolies are not legal in every country. De Beers would risk

(5) _____ in the United States, (6) _____ in Great Britain the company is free to operate without restrictive (7) _____. De Beers promotes the selling of diamonds by advertising them as an (8) _____ of personal and financial success and as a (9) _____ to love and marriage. However, De Beers' (10) _____ may soon receive a (11) _____ from two new mining companies that plan to sell diamonds outside the Central Selling Organization.

5. COLLOCATIONS

Give **two examples** of each of the following common collocations.

1. valid documents   _passport_   _birth certificate_
2. chemical compounds   _____   _____
3. criminal investigations   _____   _____
4. conventional behavior   _____   _____
5. unpopular political regimes _____   _____
6. weather predictions   _____   _____
7. optional courses   _____   _____
8. foreign currency   _____   _____
9. physical challenges   _____   _____
10. personal defense mechanisms _____   _____
11. occupational hazards   _____   _____
12. the generation gap   _____   _____
13. room dimensions   _____   _____
14. negative attitudes   _____   _____

6. WORD PARTS

pre- (before)

The prefix *pre-* means "before" in time or place.

6A Discuss with a partner the meaning of the following collocations.

precancerous growth	prefabricated house	prenuptial agreement
preconceived opinions	prehistoric remains	prerequisite course
precooked meals	premature baby	preschool children
pre-existing medical condition	premeditated murder	preshrunk T-shirt

6B Now write sentences to indicate your understanding of **five** of these collocations.

1. *My doctor found a precancerous growth on my leg, so he removed it before it caused a major problem.*

2. _____

3. _____

4. _____

5. _____

6. _____

7. WRITING

7A Writing an Advertisement

Write an advertisement for the diamond necklace in the photograph. The advertisement should be appropriate for the target market of one of the following publications:

- a women's magazine
- an elegant fashion magazine
- a general news magazine
- a sophisticated men's magazine
- a bridal magazine

7B Paragraph Writing

Write a response to **one** of the following topics. Include at least **six to eight vocabulary words** in your paragraph.

1. A monopoly is defined as a market structure for a specific product that is controlled by one company with no outside competition. In reference to De Beers and its monopoly on the marketing of diamonds, what do you think have been the positive and negative effects for the consumer?

2. What is your personal opinion and personal experience regarding the convention of giving or receiving a diamond engagement ring? What does a diamond ring mean to you? What other symbols of love and commitment might replace a diamond?

8. SPEAKING

8A Group Project: Oral Summaries

As a small group, investigate a topic related to diamonds. Topics could include the following:

- the De Beers Company
- the Central Selling Organization
- diamond mining
- the lives of diamond miners

- diamond formation
- the diamond pipeline
- the manufacture of diamond jewelry
- traditions associated with diamonds

Search the Internet for an interesting article about the topic your group has chosen. Take notes on the main ideas and supporting details. Use these notes to give an oral summary of the article's content to your group. Discuss any issues or questions that arise from the summaries. Finally, combine your group's information to give a short summary to the class about your group's topic.

8B Role-Plays

Using new vocabulary words from this chapter, act out the following role-plays.

1. You and your boyfriend/girlfriend are planning on getting married next year. You want to celebrate the engagement with a diamond ring, but your partner thinks the money could be better spent on something else, such as a honeymoon, a deposit on a house, or a new car. This is your first serious disagreement with your partner, and you do not want to cause a fight. Try to conduct a serious and reasonable discussion with your partner on this issue.

2. You have just returned from vacation in South Africa, where you visited a diamond mine. You have become aware of the dangerous working conditions and low salaries of the miners and now feel that they are being exploited by the diamond-mining companies. Your partner is planning on getting married next year, and you feel that he/she should not contribute to the wealth of the diamond regimes by buying an expensive diamond ring. Try to persuade your partner that it would be unethical to wear a diamond ring and provide some alternative solutions.

Address: http://elt.heinle.com/essentialvocab › go

For more activities related to this chapter, go to the *Essential Academic Vocabulary* website.

REVIEW

PREVIEW SENTENCES

Write **five sentences** that might describe what is happening in the photograph. Each sentence should include a **noun** and a **verb** from the following lists.

Noun	Verb
compensation	ensure
interaction	illustrate
corporation	coordinate
professional	demonstrate
promotion	maximize
goal	predict
status	generate
challenge	concentrate
commitment	communicate
revenue	undertake

1. *The professionals are predicting their company's revenue for next year.*

2. _____

3. _____

4. _____

5. _____

6. _____

1. VOCABULARY IN CONTEXT

Write the appropriate word from each group of word choices in the numbered blanks in the text.

1. considerable, initial, occupational
2. profession, professional, professionally
3. promote, promoted, promotions
4. attitudes, mechanisms, sexes
5. constraints, options, reactions
6. interactions, interactive, interacts
7. cooperate, cooperation, cooperative
8. communication, immigrant, outcome
9. components, documents, labels
10. emphasis, emphasized, emphatically
11. similar, similarity, similarly
12. demonstrate, demonstration, demonstrative
13. convention, job, location
14. ensuring, imposing, predicting
15. circumstances, dimensions, options
16. commitments, commits, committed
17. challenge, challenged, challenging
18. global, globally, globe
19. despite, hence, whereas
20. corporation, partnership, regime

THE CHANGING ROLES OF MEN AND WOMEN IN THE WORKPLACE

The workplace roles of men and women are changing as (1) _____ numbers of women continue to enter (2) _____ employment, receive (3) _____ into higher management, and start their own businesses. Although men and women are now used to working together in nearly every industry, research suggests that both (4) _____ still have different perceptions of and (5) _____ to workplace issues and (6) _____.

Today's (7) _____ business environment requires strong networking and (8) _____ skills. Although these are (9) _____ that women have traditionally (10) _____, all managers and employees are now becoming more skilled at dealing with people one-on-one. (11) _____, as organizations become more flexible, the ability to build relationships rather than issue commands—often seen as one of women's strengths—is a skill that both men and women must (12) _____ in order to succeed.

In the past, women—more often than men—tended to take time off from the (13) _____ to handle family crises, such as caring for a sick child or helping an elderly parent. These days, family leave policies for both fathers and mothers are (14) _____ that both parents have the time to bond with a new baby. Other family-friendly policies, such as flextime, are also giving mothers and fathers (15) _____ to schedule work and family (16) _____ as needed so they can share care-giving responsibilities.

The changing roles of men and women at work can be especially (17) _____ for companies active in (18) _____ markets, where gender roles may differ. (19) _____ these challenges, companies clearly benefit from the professional (20) _____ between men and women.

Adapted from William M. Pride, Robert J. Hughes, and Jack R. Kapoor, *Business,* 7th ed. (Boston: Houghton Mifflin, 2002), 310.

2. SYNONYMS

Match the verbs in column A with their meanings in column B.

	Column A		Column B
1. _____	illustrate	**a.**	give attention to a specific activity
2. _____	decline	**b.**	foretell a future event
3. _____	hypothesize	**c.**	connect
4. _____	predict	**d.**	keep out
5. _____	retain	**e.**	change
6. _____	concentrate	**f.**	produce a book
7. _____	exclude	**g.**	decrease
8. _____	imply	**h.**	make as great as possible
9. _____	link	**i.**	give a possible explanation
10. _____	maximize	**j.**	make a statement
11. _____	publish	**k.**	show the meaning by giving examples
12. _____	alter	**l.**	keep
13. _____	access	**m.**	put a plan into operation
14. _____	implement	**n.**	locate data in a computer
15. _____	comment	**o.**	communicate indirectly

3. ODD WORD OUT

Cross out the word in each line that does NOT have a similar meaning to the other three words.

1. chore, task, job, core
2. constraints, conspiracy, scheme, plot
3. objective, goal, plan, access
4. attention, convention, emphasis, stress
5. method, location, technique, manner
6. first, corresponding, initial, beginning
7. size, mechanism, measurement, dimension
8. center, core, comment, middle
9. dependence, trust, document, reliance
10. restraint, validity, restriction, constraint

4. WORD FORMS

Give the adjective forms of the following words.

Noun	Adjective	Noun	Adjective
sufficiency	*sufficient*	corporation	
ethics		profession	
globe		occupation	
specification		validity	
technology		precision	
statistics		hypothesis	
philosophy		dominancy	
interaction		circumstance	

5. COLLOCATIONS

Combine a word from column A with a word from column B to form a common collocation. Then match the two-word collocation with its definition.

Column A		Column B	
minimum	generation	series	analysis
annual	optional	courses	exercise
multinational	criminal	gap	mail
registered	statistical	investigation	age
television	physical	corporation	meeting

1. _____ a show presented every week at the same time

2. _____ a guaranteed postal delivery service

3. _____ an examination of numerical data

4. _____ the lowest age allowed for a specific activity

5. _____ classes that are not required

6. _____ a yearly convention of company managers

7. _____ active sports

8. _____ a search by police

9. _____ a large global company

10. _____ the different values of two specific age groups

6. WORD PARTS

Combine a word part from the prefix column with a word in the phrase column to complete a common collocation or expression.

*pre*_____requisite course	_____mize problems
*mini*_____mum wage	_____purpose room
_____media presentation	_____mature baby
_____bus ride	_____lingual speaker
_____nuptial agreement	_____historic remains
_____shrunk jeans	_____plex theater
_____ature railway	_____story parking garage
_____meditated murder	_____cooked food
_____lateral talks	_____fabricated house
_____school group	_____ethnic neighborhood

mini
multi
pre

Address: http://elt.heinle.com/essentialvocab ⟩ go

For more activities related to this chapter, go to the *Essential Academic Vocabulary* website.

PSYCHOLOGY

WORD LIST

Noun	Verb	Adjective	Adverb
awareness	abandon	analogous	furthermore
capacity	comprise	capable	intrinsically
conflict	convey	definite	likewise
deviation	deduce	flexible	
display	denote	fundamental	
equivalent	detect	identical	
generation	differentiate	marginal	
norm	distort	mental	
notion	evolve	modifiable	
style	exhibit	qualitative	
	facilitate		
	pose		
	reveal		
	simulate		

PREVIEW QUESTIONS

1. What kinds of emotions can you recognize on the people's faces in these photographs? Are they positive or negative emotions? How can you differentiate a positive emotion from a negative emotion?

2. How good are you at reading people's feelings from their expressions? Have you ever misread someone's expression? What was the consequence of your mistake?

3. Which facial expressions of emotions are universal? Which ones are learned through social and cultural experience?

4. Are you aware of any facial expressions that have different meanings in different cultures? Demonstrate them and explain their meanings.

5. What happens to your face when you smile? Do all smiles have the same meaning?

6. What is the connection among facial expressions, culture, and language? Do all cultures have words to express the same emotions? Is it possible to make a precise translation of emotions into another language?

READING

INNATE AND CULTURAL INFLUENCES ON EMOTIONAL EXPRESSIONS

1 Charles Darwin observed that some facial expressions seem to be universal. He proposed that these expressions are genetically determined, passed on biologically from one **generation** to the next. The facial expressions seen today, **deduced** Darwin, are those that have **evolved** to **facilitate** the communication of an emotion to another person. If someone is giving you an angry look, for
5 example, you will probably **abandon** your plan to ask for a loan.

Evidence for innate facial expressions comes from studies showing that for the most **fundamental** emotions, people in all cultures show **intrinsically** similar facial responses to **analogous** emotional stimuli. The pattern of facial movements we call a smile, for example, is universally related to positive emotions. Sadness is almost always accompanied by loose muscle
10 tone and a "long" face. **Likewise**, in almost all cultures, people **distort** their faces in an almost **identical** way when shown something they find disgusting, and a lined forehead frequently **conveys** the **notion** of frustration. Movements of the eyebrows also **denote** anger and **conflict** in almost all cultures.

Whereas some fundamental emotional expressions are innate, many others are neither innate
15 nor universal. Even innate expressions are **flexible** and **modifiable**, changing as necessary in the social contexts within which they occur. For example, facial expressions become more intense and change more frequently when people have **mental** images of social scenes rather than solitary scenes. Similarly, facial expressions in response to odors tend to be more intense when others are watching than when people are alone.
20 **Furthermore**, although a core of emotional responses is recognized by all cultures, there is a certain degree of cultural variation in recognizing some emotions. In one study, for example, Japanese and North American people agreed about which facial expressions signaled happiness, surprise, and sadness, but they frequently **revealed** disagreement about which faces showed anger,

disgust, and fear. Members of preliterate cultures, such as the Fore of New Guinea, have only a
25 **marginal awareness** of the meanings of different **styles** of facial expressions in Western cultures. In addition, people in different cultures have the **capacity** to **differentiate** emotions expressed by tone of voice. For instance, Taiwanese participants were best at **detecting** a sad tone of voice, whereas Dutch participants were best at recognizing happy tones.

As children grow, they become oriented to expressing certain emotions in **definite** ways, as
30 specified by cultural **norms**. Suppose you say, "I just bought a new car," and all your friends stick their tongues out at you. In North America, this **deviation** from the norm would mean that they are envious or resentful. But in some regions of China, such a **display** expresses surprise.

Even smiles can vary as people learn to use different **qualitative styles** to communicate certain feelings. Researchers have categorized seventeen types of smiles, including "false smiles,"
35 which fake enjoyment, and "masking smiles," which hide unhappiness. They called the smile that occurs with real happiness the *Duchenne* (pronounced "do-SHEN") *smile* after the French researcher who first noticed a difference between spontaneous, happy smiles and **posed** smiles. A genuine Duchenne smile **exhibits** contractions of the muscles around the eyes (creating a distinctive wrinkling of the skin in these areas) as well as of the muscles that raise the lips and
40 cheeks. Few people are **capable** of successfully contracting the muscles around the eyes during a **simulated** smile, so this feature can be used to differentiate "lying smiles" from genuine ones.

Physical expressions of emotion also shape how people describe them. English has over 500 emotion-related words, but some emotion words in other languages have no English **equivalent**, such as the Czech word *litost* (**comprised** of grief, sympathy, remorse, and desire) and the
45 Japanese word *ijirashii* (resulting from seeing a praiseworthy person overcoming an obstacle). Similarly, other cultures have no equivalent for some English words of emotion. The Ilongot, a Philippine headhunting group, have only one word, *liget*, for both anger and grief, while the Tahitians have words for forty-six different types of anger but no word for sadness.

Adapted from Douglas A. Bernstein, Louis A. Penner, Alison Clarke-Stewart, and Edward J. Roy, *Psychology*, 6th ed. (Boston: Houghton Mifflin, 2003), 425–27.

1. VOCABULARY IN CONTEXT

Choose the best meaning according to the context in which the word is used in the reading.

1. **deduced** (line 3)	concentrated	inferred	spoke
2. **evolved** (line 3)	developed gradually	contributed	resolved
3. **fundamental** (line 7)	constitutional	basic	adequate
4. **likewise** (line 10)	similarly	justifiably	mentally
5. **notion** (line 12)	mechanism	idea	hypothesis
6. **denote** (line 12)	represent	regulate	exclude

7.	**conflict** (line 12)	constraints	disagreement	emphasis
8.	**modifiable** (line 15)	specific	distinct	changeable
9.	**furthermore** (line 20)	distantly	additionally	considerably
10.	**revealed** (line 23)	displayed	removed	required
11.	**capacity** (line 26)	conduct	ability	category
12.	**definite** (line 29)	specific	domestic	flexible
13.	**display** (line 32)	exhibition	advertisement	document
14.	**posed** (line 37)	caused	simulated	illustrated
15.	**comprised** (line 44)	conducted	composed	commissioned

2. READING COMPREHENSION

2A Getting the Facts

1. Describe the specific facial expressions that show the following emotions (paragraph 2).

   a. positive feelings _____

   b. sadness _____

   c. disgust _____

   d. frustration _____

   e. anger _____

2. In the following cultures, describe the facial expressions or the words that describe emotions that are different from the North American norm.

   a. Fore of New Guinea _____

   b. Taiwanese _____

   c. Dutch _____

   d. Chinese _____

   e. Czechs _____

   f. Japanese _____

   g. Ilongot of the Philippines _____

   h. Tahitians _____

3. In your own words, explain how a real smile of happiness can be differentiated from a posed smile. _____

   _____

   _____

   _____

2B Making Inferences

1. Why do people display more facial expressions when they are with others than when they are alone? _____

   _____

   _____

2. How can facial expressions facilitate communication? What kinds of miscommunication may occur between people from different cultures who use facial expressions less frequently or who are expressing a different message?

   _____

   _____

3. Describe any differences in facial expressions or emotional expressions that you have observed among people from different cultures.

   _____

   _____

   _____

> It takes between five and sixteen repetitions of a word through review and practice to get it into long-term memory.

3. DICTIONARY SKILLS

Use the correct word form from the dictionary entry to complete the sentences grammatically and meaningfully.

> **de•duce** (dĭ dōos′) *tr.v.* **de•duced, de•duc•ing, de•duc•es.** To reach (a conclusion) by reasoning, especially from a general principle: *The engineers deduced from the laws of physics that the new airplane would fly.*
> **de•duct** (dĭ dŭkt′) *tr.v.* To take away (a quantity from another); subtract: *The dealer deducted the amount of our earlier deposit from the final payment for the car.*
> **de•duct•i•ble** (dĭ dŭk′tə bəl) *n.* [C; U] An amount that an owner of an insurance policy must pay on a claim before the insurance company begins to pay: *I have a $200 deductible on my health insurance.* *-adj.* Capable of being deducted, especially from one's taxable income.
> **de•duc•tion** (dĭ dŭk′shən) *n.* **1.** [C] An amount that is deducted: *a deduction from one's taxable income for medical expenses.* **2.a.** [U] The process of reaching a conclusion by reasoning, especially from general principles: *the judge's deduction that the law violated the Constitution.* **b.** [C] A conclusion reached by this process: *a brilliant deduction.*
> **de•duc•tive** (dĭ dŭk′tĭv) *adj.* Involving logical deduction: *deductive reasoning.* - **de•duc′tive•ly** *adv.*

1. This year I was able to take a tax ___deduction___ for my home business.

2. My health insurance policy covers most illnesses, but there is a $50 _____ for psychological services.

3. When you pay your rent this month, you should _____ the amount you overpaid last month.

4. Our Spanish instructor expects us to learn the rules of grammar through _____ reasoning.

5. Although I didn't tell my friend that I was having some relationship problems, she _____ that I was feeling sad.

6. In our analysis of the data, we were able to _____ some significant information.

7. The best the police can do is to make _____ from the known facts of the case.

8. Business expenses such as office supplies, telephone bills, and equipment purchases are tax _____.

9. His salary is about $35,000 before _____, making his take-home pay $29,000.

10. The professor used a _____ argument to make her point at the meeting.

4. WORD FORMS

4A Chart Completion

Complete the following chart with the different forms of each word. Note that some words do not have all forms.

Noun	Verb	Adjective	Adverb
deduction	deduce	deductive	deductively
		marginal	
		flexible	
	evolve		X
norm			
	X	fundamental	
	X	qualitative	
	X	capable	
deviation			
		detectable	X
style			

4B Word Forms in Sentences

Use the correct word form from the chart in the previous exercise to complete the following sentences. Make sure the word you choose fits meaningfully and grammatically into the sentence.

1. deduce   When I saw the sad look on Bill's face, I ____*deduced*____ that his grandfather had died.

2. marginal   In many areas of the world, people who are different from the norm in that country are _____.

3. flexible   One characteristic that employees tend to prefer in a supervisor is _____.

4. evolve   Charles Darwin is well known for his theories on _____.

5. norm   It is _____ for people to smile when they are happy.

6. fundamental   Many facial expressions appear to be _____ innate.

7. qualitative   Humanities students tend to focus more on _____ research than on quantitative research.

8. capable   Dr. Winters has a reputation as a _____ psychologist.

9. deviation   Many expressions of emotions do not _____ much from one culture to another.

10. detectable   Emotions tend to be easily _____ from people's facial expressions.

11. style   The _____ dressed woman in the advertisement has a posed smile on her face.

5. COLLOCATIONS

5A The following verbs are commonly found with specific adverbs and prepositions.

Verb	Adverb	Preposition
display	clearly, prominently, proudly	to
evolve	gradually, slowly, rapidly, naturally, independently	from, to
differentiate	clearly	between, from
deduce	easily, logically, accurately	from
deduct	automatically, weekly, monthly	from
convey	clearly, accurately, effectively, successfully	to
orient(ate)	sufficiently, correctly, politically, academically	to, toward
generate	quickly, automatically, spontaneously, internally	from

Complete each sentence with an appropriate adverb.

1. A smile **conveys** a message of happiness ___*effectively*___ to another person.

2. The psychologist **deduced** the truth _____ **from** her patient's facial expressions.

3. Most people can **differentiate** _____ **between** a real and a simulated smile.

4. A smile tends to **generate** a positive response _____ **from** another person.

5. Taxes are **deducted** _____ **from** an employee's paycheck.

6. Facial expressions **evolved** _____ **to** communicate with others.

7. The newlyweds **displayed** their happiness _____ **to** the wedding guests.

8. It usually takes some time for international students to **orient** themselves _____ **to** the new environment.

5B The following common collocations have specific meanings. Discuss these meanings. Then write **five** meaningful sentences that include some of these collocations.

a conflict of interest	a mental note	a margin of error
qualitative research	deviant behavior	a second-generation American
a vague notion	a deviation from the norm	seating capacity
a mental block	a process of deduction	identical twin

1. ___I had a <u>vague notion</u> that I'd seen that man before, but I couldn't quite remember where.___

2. _____

3. _____

4. _____

5. _____

6. _____

6. WORD PARTS

psych- (mind)

Each of the following words contains the word part *psych*, meaning "the mind." In each word, notice the word part that gives a clue about the word meaning and the suffix that indicates the part of speech. Match the words with their meanings.

psychiatric	psychodrama	psychology	psychosomatic
psychiatrist	psychological	psychopath	psychotherapy
psychobiology	psychologist		

1. _____ relating to the study and treatment of mental illness
2. _____ a medical doctor who treats people suffering from mental illness
3. _____ a person who studies the mind and its effect on behavior and emotions
4. _____ a movie or play that examines the complicated relationships of the characters
5. _____ the study of the body in relation to the mind
6. _____ relating to the way the mind works
7. _____ a way of treating someone who is mentally ill through discussion of thoughts and feelings
8. _____ someone who has a serious and permanent mental illness that causes violent or criminal behavior
9. _____ an illness caused by fear or anxiety rather than a physical problem
10. _____ the study of the mind and how it works

7. WRITING

7A Paraphrasing

See *Appendix III* for additional information on paraphrasing.

Rewrite the following sentences by using synonyms, changing the grammar structure, and changing the order of ideas. The meaning of the sentence should remain the same.

1. Charles Darwin proposed that facial expressions are genetically determined and passed on biologically from one generation to the next.

    According to Charles Darwin, expressions of the face are inherited through genes.

    _____

2. Evidence for innate facial expressions comes from studies showing that, for most fundamental emotions, people in all cultures show intrinsically similar facial responses to analogous emotional stimuli.

_____

_____

3. Whereas some fundamental emotional expressions are innate, many others are neither innate nor universal.

_____

_____

4. Facial expressions become more intense and change more frequently when people have mental images of social scenes rather than solitary scenes.

_____

_____

5. Few people are capable of successfully contracting the muscles around their eyes during a simulated smile, so this feature can be used to differentiate "lying smiles" from genuine ones.

_____

_____

6. English has over 500 emotion-related words, but some emotion words in other languages have no English equivalent.

_____

_____

7B Paragraph Writing

Write a response to **one** of the following topics. Include at least **six to eight vocabulary words** in your paragraph.

1. Advice Column

You are the writer of an advice column for a newspaper. Choose one of the letters below and write an appropriate response.

Dear Dr. Jane:
I come from a small town in Iowa, but now I'm attending a city college. I've been dating a great guy, John, for almost a year, and we are thinking about getting married when we graduate. John is an international student, but until recently we'd never had any intercultural conflicts. Now there's a problem, though. John's parents are coming to visit next month and, apparently, they are not pleased that he is dating an American. John thinks I should stay out of the way while his parents are here, but I feel that his parents need to get to know me if we are going to have a future together. I'm really afraid that this problem is going to ruin our relationship. Please give me some advice.

Heartsick in California

Dear Dr. Tom:
I've been struggling financially to get through college, and I rely on my campus job to help pay for expenses. I've been working in this job for six months, and I got a promotion last month to a better position with more money. Unfortunately, my new boss doesn't seem to like me. He always gives me nasty looks, never smiles, and barely says a word to me. He's totally inflexible as well. Last week my car broke down, and I arrived late. He almost fired me, even though I had called to tell him the problem. I think he's being totally unfair, and I'm sure he'll find some way to get rid of me. I need to keep this job to pay for my rent. What can I do to keep this job and make my boss like me?

Desperate in Ohio

2. Character Description

English has over 500 emotion-related words, some of which are listed here. Think about a person you know who is very emotional. Write five words of emotion that you associate with this person. Then write a paragraph in which you describe how this person demonstrates these emotional characteristics. Add specific details to illustrate how these emotions were triggered.

anger	disgust	grief	nostalgia	sorrow
anxiety	dislike	happiness	pain	sympathy
apathy	dismay	hate	pleasure	threat
contentment	elation	irritation	pride	unhappiness
despair	excitement	joy	sadness	guilt
disappointment	fear	love	shame	discontent

8. Speaking

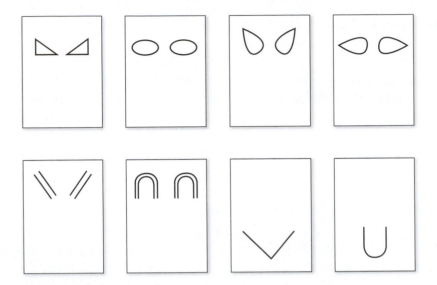

Adapted from Douglas A. Bernstein, Louis A. Penner, Alison Clarke-Stewart, and Edward J. Roy, *Psychology*, 6th ed. (Boston: Houghton Mifflin, 2003), 426.

8A Conducting a Survey

Certain geometric patterns are common to threatening masks in many cultures. Go to a public place in your college, such as a cafeteria or a campus park, and ask ten people to participate in your survey. Show them the chart of geometric patterns illustrated above and ask them to choose which member of each pair is more threatening.

Tabulate the results below; then summarize your findings briefly to the class. Compare and contrast the findings of your classmates.

1. _____

2. _____

3. _____

4. _____

5. _____

6. _____

7. _____

8. _____

9. _____

10. _____

8B Pair Discussion: Physical, Emotional, and Verbal Reactions

Some facial expressions are innate and predictable. Others vary according to the social and cultural situation. Discuss with a partner your physical, emotional, and verbal reactions to the following images or situations. Make the appropriate facial expressions to display your emotions clearly.

seeing a rat	smelling freshly cut grass
meeting a cute baby	seeing a puppy
smelling old eggs	being bitten by a mosquito
failing an exam	announcing a wedding
receiving a gift	listening to a sad story
watching a horror movie	showing anger
hearing that someone has died	showing disappointment that you did not win the prize
seeing a snake	reporting a car accident
feeling a spider on your back	smelling popcorn
smelling a good meal	asking for a loan

Address: http://elt.heinle.com/essentialvocab › go

For more activities related to this chapter, go to the *Essential Academic Vocabulary* website.

CHAPTER 12

HISTORY

WORD LIST

Noun		Verb	Adjective	Adverb
contact	instability	accommodate	dynamic	implicitly
emigration	motivation	assign	ideological	ultimately
enhancement	network	dispose	manual	
estate	perspective	enable	medical	
expansion	pursuit	enforce	radical	
exploitation	revolution	exceed	subordinate	
exposure	survival	sustain	underlying	
hierarchy	transformation		visible	
incentive	transition			
incidence	transportation			
input				

PREVIEW QUESTIONS

1. What was the Industrial Revolution? Where and when did it take place?

2. Before the Industrial Revolution, what kind of work did most poor people do and where did they live? What happened to these people when the Industrial Revolution began?

3. What changes in society happened during the Industrial Revolution? How did it change the way people lived?

4. What were working conditions like at this time? Give examples of how and where men, women, and children worked.

5. What were some consequences of the Industrial Revolution for rich people and for poor people?

READING

THE IMPACT OF THE INDUSTRIAL REVOLUTION

1 Although inventions were the most **visible** and **dynamic** aspects of the Industrial **Revolution** in Europe, many other **transformations** in the **hierarchies** of society, politics, **transportation**, and the economy took place. These early changes—including smoky cities, slum neighborhoods, polluted water, child **manual** labor in mines and textile mills—transformed entire regions into
5 industrial landscapes.

The most dramatic environmental changes brought about by industrialization occurred in the **expansion** of urban areas in Europe. London, one of the largest cities in 1700 with 500,000 inhabitants, grew to 959,000 by 1800 and **exceeded** 2,363,000 by 1850, by then the largest city in the world. Smaller towns grew even faster. Manchester's population increased eightfold in a
10 century. Liverpool grew sixfold in the first 60 years of the nineteenth century.

People who benefited greatly from the **transition** to industrialization poured their new wealth into fine country **estates**, new homes, churches, museums, and theaters and lived comfortable lives, out of **contact** with the workers, who lived in dangerous, overcrowded, and unhealthy conditions. As poor migrants streamed in from the countryside, developers
15 **accommodated** their need for housing by building cheap row houses for the migrants to rent. Often, several families had to live in one small room. People **disposed** of their sewage and trash by throwing it out the windows to be washed down the streets. The poor kept pigs and chickens, the rich kept horses, and pedestrians stepped into the street at their own risk. Air pollution from burning coal got steadily worse. People drank water drawn from wells and rivers contaminated by
20 sewage and industrial runoff.

To the long list of preindustrial diseases such as smallpox, dysentery, and tuberculosis, industrialization added **exposure** to new **medical** problems. Rickets, a bone disease caused by a lack of sunshine, became common in the dark and smoky industrial cities. Steamships brought cholera from India, causing great epidemics that struck the residents of poor neighborhoods
25 especially hard. In the 1850s, when the average life expectancy in England was 40 years, it was only 24 years in Manchester, and around 17 years in Manchester's poorest neighborhoods because of the high **incidence** of infant mortality.

Most industrial jobs at this time were unskilled and repetitive, and work regulations were not strictly **enforced**. Workdays were long with few breaks, and industrial accidents were common
30 and could ruin a family. Workers who performed one simple task over and over had little sense of **motivation** or connection to the final product. Unlike even the poorest preindustrial farmer or artisan, factory workers were always **subordinate** to the bosses and had no **input** over their tools, jobs, or working hours and thus had little **incentive** beyond mere **survival**.

Women workers were concentrated in textile mills, earning one-third to one-half as much as
35 men. Young unmarried women worked to support themselves or to save for marriage. Married women took factory jobs when their husbands were unable to support the family. Mothers of infants faced a hard choice: whether to keep their babies with wet nurses at great expense or bring them to the factory and keep them quiet with opiates. Rather than working together as a family **network**, husbands and wives increasingly worked in different places.

40 Even with both parents working, poor families found it hard to **sustain** even the most basic level of life. As in preindustrial societies, the **perspective** of parents was that children should contribute to their upkeep as soon as they were capable. The first generation of workers brought their children with them to the factories and mines as early as age five or six; they had little choice since there were no public schools or daycare centers. Employers **enabled**, and even
45 **implicitly** encouraged, this practice because children were cheaper and more obedient than adults and, because of their size, could be **assigned** to tie broken threads or crawl under machines to sweep the dust. Mine operators also used children to pull coal carts along the low passageways.

Changes as **radical** as the Industrial Revolution could not occur without **underlying** political **instability** and **ideological** conflict, which **ultimately** led to workers' protests and strikes for the
50 end of **exploitation** and for the **enhancement** of working conditions. Another response to the hard conditions was **emigration**. Between 1830 and 1890, approximately 10 million Europeans emigrated to the United States in **pursuit** of a better life.

Adapted from Richard W. Bulliet, Pamela Kyle Crossley, Daniel R. Headrick, Steven W. Hirsch, Lyman J. Johnson, and David Northrup, *The Earth and Its Peoples: A Global History,* 2nd ed. (Boston: Houghton Mifflin, 2003), 471–74.

1. VOCABULARY IN CONTEXT

Determine how the boldface words are used in the reading. Then for each item, choose the word or phrase that is closest in meaning.

1. _____ **transformation** (line 2)
   a. movement
   b. change
   c. removal

2. _____ **expansion** (line 7)
   a. structure
   b. creation
   c. increase

3. _____ **exposure** (line 22)
   a. photograph
   b. direction
   c. danger

4. _____ **incidence** (line 27)
   a. rate
   b. event
   c. evolution

5. _____ **input** (line 32)

   a. control

   b. information

   c. notion

6. _____ **incentive** (line 33)

   a. awareness

   b. capacity

   c. motivation

7. _____ **perspective** (line 41)

   a. situation

   b. condition

   c. attitude

8. _____ **ultimately** (line 49)

   a. primarily

   b. finally

   c. really

9. _____ **enhancement** (line 50)

   a. orientation

   b. quality

   c. improvement

10. _____ **pursuit** (line 52)

   a. search

   b. activity

   c. achievement

2. READING COMPREHENSION

2A Getting the Facts

1. Circle any topics that are NOT discussed in the reading, "The Impact of the Industrial Revolution."

- child labor
- housing conditions
- population shifts
- political beliefs
- medical problems

- manual labor
- family size
- working conditions for women
- emigration
- the causes of the Industrial Revolution

2. Which of the following three cities had the largest population in the world in 1850?

London   Manchester   Liverpool

3. According to the article, workers lived in "dangerous, overcrowded, and unhealthy conditions" (lines 13 and 14). Find at least one fact in the third paragraph to support each of these conditions.

   a. dangerous _____

   b. overcrowded _____

   c. unhealthy _____

4. List three facts from the reading about each of the following groups of people.

factory owners	1.
	2.
	3.
male workers	1.
	2.
	3.
unmarried female workers	1.
	2.
	3.
married female workers	1.
	2.
	3.
children	1.
	2.
	3.

5. What were two consequences of worker dissatisfaction during the Industrial Revolution?

a. _____

b. _____

2B Making Inferences

1. According to the reading, life expectancy was 40 years in London but only 17 years in the worst neighborhoods of Manchester. What can you infer about Manchester from these facts?

_____

_____

2. How did the type of work done by workers in factories and mines impact workers' health?

_____

_____

3. What can you infer about working conditions in the United States during this time period?

_____

_____

> It is not enough to know only a word's meaning. You also need to know its pronunciation, spelling, grammatical patterns, collocations, associations, connotations, and related word forms.

3. DICTIONARY SKILLS

Study the dictionary entry for *contact*. Complete the sentences with the appropriate collocations.

> **con•tact** (**kŏn′**tăkt′) *n.* **1.** [U] The touching or coming together of persons or things: *Don't let the chemicals come in contact with your skin.* **2.** [U] The condition of being in communication: *We lost contact with our former neighbors after they moved.* **3.** [C] A person who is in a position to be of help; a connection: *His uncle has numerous contacts in the government.* **4.** [C] **a.** A connection between two conductors that allows an electric current to flow. **b.** A part or device that makes or breaks a connection in an electrical circuit: *the contacts of a switch.* **5.** [C] A contact lens: *Have you seen my contacts? -v.* (**kŏn′**tăkt′ *or* kən **tăkt′**). *-tr.* **1.** To bring (sthg.) into contact with sthg. else; touch: *If water contacts the paper, it will leave a mark.* **2.** To get in touch with (sbdy.); communicate with: *The salesman contacted several customers by telephone. -intr.* To be or come into contact: *Bare wires that contact might cause a fire.*

business contacts	contact sports	face-to-face contact
contact information	electrical contact	loss of contact
contact lenses	established contact	physical contact
contact number		

1. My desk light is not working. There seems to be a problem with the _____.

2. These days, many people who have visual problems prefer to wear _____ rather than glasses.

3. American football and rugby are examples of _____, in which players are allowed to touch each other when they are trying to get the ball.

4. Janet hasn't yet made _____ with her new online friend, but they e-mail each other every day.

5. Some cultures demonstrate their affection through _____, while other cultures prefer not to touch.

6. David Brown made a lot of useful _____ at the marketing conference he attended last week.

7. Donna Jones has been doing business in Asia for many years, so she has a lot of _____ there who always help her when she visits.

8. My coworker gave me her _____ in case I need to discuss an important work issue over the weekend.

9. The pilot reported _____ with air traffic control at the airport, but he was able to land the plane safely.

10. When I started my new job, I had to fill out a form listing all my _____, including my telephone number and e-mail address.

4. WORD FORMS

4A Chart Completion

Complete the chart with the corresponding noun or verb forms.

Noun	Verb
enforcement	enforce
pursuit	
	sustain
survival, survivor	
	contact
transformation	
	emigrate
transportation	
	motivate
expansion	
	exploit
revolution	
	input

4B Word Forms in Sentences

Create **five** new sentences about the impact of industrialization, including a **noun** and a **verb** from the chart in the previous exercise in each sentence.

1. _The expansion of industry in the nineteenth century caused factory owners to exploit their workers._

2. _____

_____

3. _____

_____

4. _____

_____

5. _____

_____

6. _____

_____

5. COLLOCATIONS

5A The following nouns are typically found in combination with specific verbs. Match the nouns with the verbs to make meaningful phrases.

immigrants	regulations	the speed limit
the law	resources	workers

exploit   _workers_   enforce   _____

               _____   _____

               _____   _____

a career	a criminal	growth
happiness	injuries	life

pursue   _____   sustain   _____

              _____   _____

              _____   _____

5B Match the situations in the following sentences with the collocations that describe them.

group dynamics	press exposure	tax incentives
ideological differences	public transportation	transitional government
medical advice	survival rate	ultimate responsibility
mood enhancers		

1. _____ I don't have my own car, so I take the train or bus to work.

2. _____ The way that people work together can be very important.

3. _____ Some people use alcohol or drugs to feel better.

4. _____ After the revolution, a new group of politicians ruled the country until elections could take place.

5. _____ The doctor told Jim to rest and drink plenty of liquids until he feels better.

6. _____ Jennifer and Susan used to be close friends, but now they rarely see each other because they do not agree on political and social issues.

7. _____ Refunds from the government are meant to encourage businesses to expand.

8. _____ In the past, most people died of cancer, but today many people recover and lead normal lives.

9. _____ The marriage of the two movie stars was widely reported in the media.

10. _____ The president makes the final decisions about how the company operates.

6. WORD PARTS

trans- (across, changed)

The prefix *trans-* means "across" or "changed."

6A Match the verbs in the left column to the item that is moved or altered in the right column.

1. _____	transfer	a.	heart
2. _____	transform	b.	book
3. _____	translate	c.	business
4. _____	transmit	d.	electronic messages
5. _____	transplant	e.	environment
6. _____	transport	f.	grades
7. _____	transact	g.	goods
8. _____	transfuse	h.	blood

6B Make the following verbs into nouns by adding the appropriate noun suffix endings where needed.

Verb	Noun
transfuse	
transport	
transform	
transmit	
transact	
translate	
transplant	
transfer	

7. WRITING

7A Writing a Summary

See *Appendix IV* for additional information on summarizing.

Reread the article "The Impact of the Industrial Revolution" OR find an article about the Industrial Revolution on the Internet. Take notes in your own words about the main ideas in the text and use your notes to summarize the reading. Include at least **six to eight vocabulary words** in your summary.

7B Paragraph Writing

Write a response to **one** of the following topics about living in the time of the Industrial Revolution. Include at least **six to eight vocabulary words** in your paragraph.

1. You are a young married woman with three children under the age of six. You have recently moved to Manchester with your husband and children to find work in the textile factories. Describe a day in your new life, adding details about your housing situation, your job and your husband's job, the problems of childcare, and your concerns about the unhealthy environment you now have to live in. Compare this situation with your former life in a small farming village. Have you made the right decision in moving to Manchester?

2. You are a young unmarried man. You have been working in the coal mines of northern England for ten years (since you were a child of ten), and you are very dissatisfied with your present life. You have recently become involved with labor conflicts, and you are now on strike trying to enhance the working conditions for the coal miners in your region. You are considering the possibility of emigrating to the United States, where you hope you would find a better life. Write a letter to your parents in the countryside describing your working conditions and explain to them why you are thinking about emigrating.

8. SPEAKING

8A A Cooperative Learning Research Project

As a small group, choose a topic related to the Industrial Revolution to research. Topics could include the following:

- the causes of the Industrial Revolution
- child labor
- housing conditions
- population shifts
- working in a coal mine

- working in a textile mill
- health problems
- transportation
- working conditions for women
- emigration

Individually, search the Internet for one or two interesting articles about the topic your group has chosen. Read each own article several times and take notes on the main ideas and the supporting details.

Using only brief notes, each group member should give a short oral summary about the content of the article to the whole group. Group members should ask questions and discuss issues raised in each presentation.

Finally, as a group, prepare a short oral summary of the key information about your topic collected from all group members and present it to the entire class.

8B Role-Plays

Using new vocabulary words from this chapter, act out the following role-plays.

1. You are discussing with a friend the ethics of buying cheap clothing from large discount stores. There are ideological differences between you and your friend regarding this issue. From your perspective, purchasing these clothes contributes to the exploitation of poor workers in developing countries. On the other hand, your friend believes that the global economy actually enhances the lives and income level of the workers who produce the clothes. Support each opinion with specific examples.

2. You are a young married man with a promising career in advertising. Your wife is a journalist with a major newspaper. You and your wife are expecting your first child in a few months, and you are faced with the difficult issue of childcare. You both know that good childcare is expensive and difficult to find. You are considering the possibility of one of you working part-time to take good care of the baby, but you have not yet decided who will give up the full-time job. Try to resolve this issue with your wife by figuring out who is going to stay at home with the baby.

Address: http://elt.heinle.com/essentialvocab   › go

For more activities related to this chapter, go to the *Essential Academic Vocabulary* website.

WHAT'S THE FOOL DOING? I DISTINCTLY TOLD HIM TO **LIE** IN FRONT OF THE CAMERA!!!

CHAPTER 13

POLITICAL SCIENCE

WORD LIST

Noun	Verb	Adjective	Adverb	Preposition
channel	acknowledge	alternative	primarily	via
discretion	aid	biased	somewhat	
domain	allocate	contrary		
equipment	extract	interventionist		
fee	ignore	liberal		
infrastructure	substitute	neutral		
interval	tape	overseas		
presumption		virtual		
priority				
protocol				
publication				
ratio				
rationalization				
scope				
transmission				
trend				

PREVIEW QUESTIONS

1. Do you vote in local and national elections? Explain why you choose to vote or not to vote.

2. How do you choose which political candidate to vote for?

3. Which type of media influences you the most to vote for particular issues or candidates?

4. How can you evaluate whether the information you see or hear about political candidates is true?

5. In your opinion, should there be limits on the money political candidates can spend during an election campaign?

6. What do you know about election campaigns in other countries? How do you get this information?

7. How do you think political campaigns might change in the future?

READING

POLITICAL CAMPAIGNS AND THE MEDIA

1 Preparing a political campaign requires a specific **protocol** for raising funds and developing a strategy; in both cases, modern technologies are **acknowledged** to play an increasingly important role. Carrying out the campaign is now done **primarily via** the media. To understand the role of media in modern politics, it is important to understand the history of media as a business
5 enterprise, the consequent dependency on attracting as large an audience for their advertisers as possible, and the effect this need has had on the **domain** of political news, including political campaigns. Parties and candidates gain access to the media via legally required free time, paid advertising, free news coverage, and direct-contact media, such as direct mailings, telephone calls, and e-mail lists. The **priorities** of media reporters and publishers are to use political news to
10 attract as large an audience as possible and also to meet the demands of the media owners, who may have specific political agendas of their own. An increasing **trend**, especially in the United States, in the use of **alternative** media, such as the Internet and cable television, involves gathering a large portion of political information from paid ads.

Remarkable new technologies and **infrastructures** are now in place to **aid** the spread of
15 communications of all forms. Communications satellites, first used to present the news in the 1980s, are now being launched at the rate of over 80 new systems per year. Fiber-optic cables are providing even better quality and more accessible two-way communication capability. Digital compression makes it possible to have more **channels** in the same radio frequency space and is much cheaper than sending programs by satellite. The Internet provides "**virtual** television" as
20 well as printed political news. Cable television has shown remarkable growth and diversity, ranging in **scope** from **liberal** or fundamentalist programming to the unhurried, carefully balanced, and **noninterventionist** direct reporting of C-SPAN. Fax machines, satellite television, computer modems, and radio talk shows have come to China and other nations where only a few years ago color television was a rarity. The Pan African News Agency, located in Senegal on the
25 west coast of Africa, has installed satellite and Internet communications systems to **substitute** for

telegraph and radio **transmissions** that were often interrupted by desert dust storms or heavy rains. The telecommunications industries of the European states are also coordinating their own information highways.

There is a **presumption** that any group, anywhere, should be able to reach any **overseas**
30   location with the new technologies. However, not all political parties have enough finances **allocated** to use this technology, and not all citizens can access it. Citizen response to political news is heavily influenced by economic and social limits to access, and the disparities are great. Internet use is an example: As of January 2001, the **ratio** of American households with personal computers compared to those without was 4 to 1, and 100 million people were online; however,
35   in Africa only 11 of the continent's 43 nations had full Internet service, and even in those nations, access was severely limited by poor or nonexistent phone service, while in China the **fees** for the installation of telephone **equipment** can still reach as high as $600.

We ourselves seldom know how the media is affecting us. There is considerable evidence that U.S. citizens rely heavily on candidates' ads to "get some sense of what a candidate is like"; when
40   asked, 62 percent either completely or mostly agree that "I often don't become aware of political candidates until I see their advertising on television." On the other hand, 74 percent say that news reports give them a better idea of where a candidate stands on the issues than do ads, and 65 percent prefer news reports to **taped** ads for getting an "idea of what a candidate is like personally." Those with Internet access can sample candidate and party Web pages, but many
45   apparently do so only to **extract rationalizations** for their support of a candidate while **ignoring contrary** information.

Although those who pay attention to media coverage of campaigns tend to be better educated and more interested and active in politics, they do not appear to remember much of what they watch, hear, or read. Studies in which television viewers have been interviewed show
50   extremely limited recall. After an **interval** of two hours, viewers of a television network news show can normally remember only one of the twenty or so stories usually presented. News stories that focus on personalities and domestic news items are "better recognized and better recalled than standard political news." In the United States, citizens do **somewhat** better at retaining personal information about candidates, and they remember best of all favorable information
55   about the candidates they prefer.

Thus, although it is obviously true that the media are a powerful force in shaping our ideas about the nature of political reality, political scientists have a long way to go in determining how much influence the media really have and the best ways to channel it. For the consumers of media information, it is important to remember that political news is rarely, if ever, **neutral**
60   because the content of media **publications** is almost always **biased** in some way at the **discretion** of the publisher.

Adapted from Kay Lawson, *The Human Polity: A Comparative Introduction to Political Science,* 5th ed. (Boston: Houghton Mifflin, 2003), 239–41, 248–49.

1. VOCABULARY IN CONTEXT

Determine how the words in column A are used in the reading. Then choose a word in column B that is closest in meaning.

	Column A		Column B
1._____	primarily (line 3)	a.	period of time
2._____	via (line 3)	b.	not supporting either side
3._____	domain (line 6)	c.	tendency
4._____	trend (line 11)	d.	satisfactory, but invented, explanations
5._____	infrastructures (line 14)	e.	mainly
6._____	virtual (line 19)	f.	proportion
7._____	substitute (line 25)	g.	opposite
8._____	allocated (line 31)	h.	area of interest or activity
9._____	ratio (line 33)	i.	payment
10._____	fees (line 36)	j.	by means of
11._____	rationalizations (line 45)	k.	simulated
12._____	contrary (line 46)	l.	basic systems for communication
13._____	interval (line 50)	m.	prejudiced
14._____	neutral (line 59)	n.	use in place of something else
15._____	biased (line 60)	o.	set aside for a particular purpose

2. READING COMPREHENSION

2A Getting the Facts

1. Complete the chart by listing the features of each new technology mentioned in the second paragraph.

Technology	Features
communications satellites	*over 80 new systems launched per year*
fiber-optic cables	
digital compression	
the Internet	
cable television	

2. What facts did you learn about the communications systems of countries on the following continents?

   a. Asia _____

   _____

   b. Africa _____

   _____

   c. Europe _____

   _____

3. Scan the reading for the following numbers, percentages, and dates. Write them on the blank preceding each appropriate statement.

62 percent	$600	74 percent	100 million	65 percent
about 20	1980s	80+	11	43

   a. _____ the cost of installing a telephone in China

   b. _____ the percentage of people who don't know much about candidates until they see political ads on television

   c. _____ the number of countries in Africa

   d. _____ when the first satellites were used to present news

   e. _____ the number of Internet users in the U.S. in 2001

   f. _____ the percentage of people who think that news reports do a better job than advertisements at stating a candidate's opinion on the issues

   g. _____ the number of new satellite systems launched each year

   h. _____ the number of African countries with complete Internet service

   i. _____ the percentage of people who believe that ads do a worse job than news reports in conveying a candidate's personality

   j. _____ the approximate number of stories presented on a single network news show

4. Indicate whether the following statements are true (T) or false (F) about the studies in the fifth paragraph that describe the recall ability of television viewers.

   a. _____ Viewers tend to remember stories that emphasize political issues.

   b. _____ Americans tend to recall positive information about their favorite candidates.

   c. _____ Television viewers remember most of the stories they see on news shows.

   d. _____ A news item about a movie star would probably be better remembered than an overseas political report.

   e. _____ Political information about a candidate is not recalled as well as personal information.

2B Making Inferences

1. Give examples to illustrate the meanings of the following methods that political parties and candidates use to gain access to the media.

   a. legally required free time _____

   b. paid advertising _____

   c. free news coverage _____

   d. direct-contact media _____

2. What can you infer about the possible reasons for the limited recall of political news by television viewers in the United States?

   _____

   _____

3. Political advertising via technological media is currently less available in some areas of the world. What impact might this have on politics and voting?

   _____

   _____

> You remember only 10–15 percent of words you hear or read only once. By developing effective strategies for reviewing words at steadily increasing intervals, word recall is increased.

3. DICTIONARY SKILLS

Study the dictionary entry for the word *neutral*. Define the following phrases or provide an example for each one.

> **neu•tral** (noo′trəl) *adj.* **1.a.** Not supporting either side in a war, dispute, or contest: *a neutral nation.* **b.** Not belonging to either side in a conflict: *neutral territory.* **2.** Describing a color, such as gray, black, beige, or white, that lacks strong hue: *I bought a neutral-colored coat that goes with all of my clothes.* **3.** Without definite or distinctive characteristics: *a neutral flavor.* **4.** In chemistry, neither acid nor alkaline: *a neutral solution.* **5.** Having positive electric charges exactly balanced by negative electric charges: *a neutral atom.* *-n.* [U] A position (especially in a vehicle) in which gears are not engaged, so no power can be transmitted: *Leave the car in neutral while I check the engine.*

1. a neutral-colored car _____

2. a neutral country _____

3. a neutral flavor _____

4. a neutral substance _____

5. in neutral gear _____

6. neutral territory _____

7. a neutral opinion _____

8. neutral particles _____

9. a neutral policy _____

10. a neutral expression _____

4. WORD FORMS IN SENTENCES

Complete the following sentences using the grammatically correct form of the word in italics. (It may be necessary to change a verb form or tense or to make a noun plural.)

1. Media reporters _____ news in order to attract as large an audience as possible.
   priority, prioritize, prior

2. In Senegal, outdated communications systems have been _____ with satellite and Internet systems.
   substitution, substitute

3. To _____ a residence in China with a telephone system is very expensive.
   equipment, equip

4. Switzerland is a country that has retained its _____ for many years.
   neutrality, neutralize, neutral

5. Senator Edward Kennedy is well known for his _____ political ideas.
   liberalism, liberalize, liberal, liberally

6. Before the election, this candidate was _____ unknown to the public.
   virtual, virtually

7. Many citizens say they are _____ of the political policies of the candidates in a local election.
   ignorance, ignore, ignorant, ignorantly

8. The _____ of funds for advertising is not nearly large enough to produce positive results.
   allocation, allocate

9. Voters do not always make _____ choices because they concentrate more on a candidate's personality than on the candidate's policies.
   rationalization, rationalize, rational, rationally

10. All political parties issue _____ to spread information about their candidates.
    publisher, publication, publish

5. COLLOCATIONS

5A In the space provided, write the word that can precede all four words in each group to form common collocations.

liberal	neutral	overseas	published	rational

1. _____ assignment, markets, work, travel
2. _____ opinion, argument, explanation, idea
3. _____ arts, party, politics, policies
4. _____ country, territory, color, taste
5. _____ papers, magazine, journal, statement

acknowledged	alternative	biased	somewhat	virtual

6. _____ report, opinion, publication, media
7. _____ expert, genius, artist, government
8. _____ tired, sleepy, better, hungry
9. _____ reality, shopping, banking, conference
10. _____ medicine, energy, media, lifestyle

5B Using collocations from exercise A, write nine sentences that clearly illustrate the meanings of the collocations.

1. _Alternative medicine, using herbs and plants to cure illnesses, has become much more popular in recent years._

2. _____

3. _____

4. _____

5. _____

6. _____

7. _____

_____

8. _____

_____

9. _____

_____

10. _____

_____

6. WORD PARTS

Adjective Suffixes

6A The suffixes in the chart are common adjective endings. Add two adjectives with the same suffix to each row in the chart.

Adjective Suffixes	Examples
-al	chemical, manual, legal, annual,
-ative, -ive	active, creative, attractive, talkative,
-ent/-ant	evident, dependent, constant, apparent,
-ic	athletic, classic, ethnic, poetic,
-ish	childish, foolish, selfish, babyish,
-ous, ious	ambiguous, humorous, delicious, nervous,
-able	considerable, capable, favorable, comfortable,

6B You attended a lecture last week by Dr. James Smithton, a visiting professor, and you want to describe the lecture to a friend. Fill in the blanks with appropriate adjectives from the chart.

1. The lecture was _____.
2. Dr. Smithton was _____.
3. His voice was _____.
4. His appearance was _____.
5. His interaction with the audience was _____.
6. The topic of the lecture was _____.

7. The details and examples were _____.

8. The person sitting next to me was _____.

9. The questions after the lecture were _____.

10. At the reception afterward, the snacks were _____.

7. WRITING

7A Writing a Speech

You have been assigned to introduce Shirley Rodrigues, a Democratic candidate for mayor in the local election in your town, at a political meeting that will be attended by members of the community and the local media. You have been given a few notes about her and must prepare a short introduction outlining her achievements and the reasons she is the best candidate for the position. Add **two** additional details, using words from this chapter. Arrange the information from these notes in a logical and interesting way.

- ➤ acknowledged expert in economics
- ➤ received allocations of funding for various community projects in the past
- ➤ cooperative team member
- ➤ close relationships with her colleagues
- ➤ political interests are broad in scope
- ➤ knowledgeable about how to make use of alternative media
- ➤ able to channel people's energy in the right direction
- ➤ helped to build communications infrastructure in this town
- ➤ has worked extensively overseas
- ➤ political publications well known in the community
- ➤ _____
- ➤ _____

Today I'm pleased to introduce Shirley Rodrigues, who _____

_____

_____

_____

_____

_____

Let us all support Ms. Rodrigues in her pursuit of the position of mayor in this town.

7B Paragraph Writing

Write a response to **one** of the following topics. Include at least **six to eight vocabulary words** in your paragraph.

1. What politician, past or present, from any country, do you admire the most? What was the politician's position and political party affiliation? Why do you admire this person? Write a biographical paragraph that describes this person's contributions to the national or global political environment.

2. Watch a television news show or listen to a radio news program, focusing on a political ad or a story that describes a political event or a politician. Take notes as you listen and evaluate the information for its accuracy and emotional appeal. Write a paragraph summarizing the ad or story. At the end of the summary, state your opinion about whether the information presented was neutral or biased in a specific way and for what purpose.

8. SPEAKING

8A Partner Activity: Explaining a Political Cartoon

Find a political cartoon that you understand in a magazine, a newspaper, or on the Internet. Explain the content of the cartoon to a partner. Include any necessary background information, such as political events, political party, and political personalities, so that your partner can understand the cartoon and appreciate its humor. Add your observations about the following:

- the type of media in which the cartoon appeared
- the political bias of the publication
- the style of drawing
- the message in the text
- emotional appeal
- tone and style
- the type of humor
- the accuracy of the message

8B Group Discussion: Voting Rates

In the United States, only about half of the registered voters participate in national elections. Compared to other countries and political systems, this is a very low rate. In small groups, discuss some possible reasons for low voter turnout and compare this information to that of other countries you know. How might the following factors influence the rate of voting?

- educational level of voters
- minimum age of voter registration
- age of voter
- marital status
- income level
- ethnic group
- attitude toward politics
- access to voting location
- hours of voting
- level of interest in the candidates
- political party affiliation

Address: http://elt.heinle.com/essentialvocab   ❯ go

For more activities related to this chapter, go to the *Essential Academic Vocabulary* website.

LINGUISTICS

WORD LIST

Noun	Verb	Adjective	Adverb	Conjunction
adaptation	cite	abstract	inherently	notwithstanding
bond	devote	accurate	nevertheless	
clause	incorporate	ambiguous		
colleague	infer	brief		
conclusion	manipulate	complex		
debate	unify	incompatible		
device	violate	isolated		
expert		minimal		
format		mutual		
instruction		ongoing		
intelligence		preliminary		
maturity		unique		
summary				

PREVIEW QUESTIONS

1. What do linguists study?

2. How can you define language? What is the role of grammar in language?

3. What linguistic problems have you experienced in learning a foreign or second language?

4. How do animals communicate with each other? Give some specific examples of animal communication.

5. How is animal communication different from human communication?

6. What kinds of animals have been taught to communicate with humans? What methods have they used to communicate? How successful have they been?

READING

CAN NONHUMANS USE LANGUAGE?

1   Some linguists say that it is the ability of humans to acquire and use language that differentiates them from all other animals. Yet other animals, too, use symbols to communicate. Bees perform a dance that tells other bees where they found sources of nectar; the grunts and gestures of chimpanzees signify varying desires and emotions. These forms of communication do not
5   necessarily have the grammatical characteristics of language, however. **Notwithstanding** these obvious differences, some **experts** have **devoted** many years of their careers to **ongoing** studies of the linguistic capabilities of animals.

Over the last forty years, several researchers have asserted that nonhumans can master language. Chimpanzees and gorillas have been the most popular targets of study because at
10   **maturity** they are estimated to have the **intelligence** of two- or three-year-old children, who are usually well on their way to learning language. Dolphins, too, have been studied because they have a **complex** communication system and exceptionally large brains relative to their body size. It would seem that if these animals were unable to learn language, their general intelligence could not be blamed. Instead, failure would be attributed to the absence of a genetic makeup that
15   permits language learning.

The question of whether nonhuman mammals can learn to use language is not a simple one, for at least two reasons. First, language is more than just communication, but defining just when animals are exhibiting that "something more" is a source of **debate.** What seems to differentiate human language from the gestures, grunts, chirps, whistles, or cries of other animals is
20   grammar—a formal set of rules for combining words. Also, because of their anatomical structures, nonhuman mammals will never be able to "speak" in the same way that humans do. To test these animals' ability to learn language, investigators, therefore, must devise innovative ways for them to communicate.

David and Ann Premack taught their chimp, Sarah, to communicate by placing differently
25   shaped chips, each symbolizing a word, on a magnetic board (1971). Lana, a chimpanzee studied by Duane Rumbaugh (1977), learned to follow **instructions** to communicate by pressing keys on a specially designed computer. American Sign Language (ASL), the hand-gesture language used by deaf people, has been used by Beatrice and Allen Gardner with the chimp Washoe and by Herbert Terrace with Nim Chimsky. And Kanzi, a bonobo (commonly known as a pygmy

30 chimpanzee) studied by Sue Savage-Rumbaugh (1990, 1993), learned to recognize spoken words and to communicate by both gesturing and pressing word-symbol keys on a computer that would "speak" for him.

Studies of these animals suggested that they could spontaneously **manipulate** combinations of words to refer to things that were not present. Washoe, Lana, Sarah, Nim, and Kanzi all
35 mastered between 130 and 500 words. Their vocabulary included names for concrete objects such as *apple* or *me*; verbs such as *tickle* and *eat*; adjectives such as *happy* and *big*; and adverbs such as *again*. The animals **incorporated** the words into sentences, expressing wishes such as "You tickle me" or "If Sarah good, then apple." Sometimes the sentences referred to things in the past. Finally, all these animals seemed to enjoy their communication **devices** and used them
40 spontaneously to interact and form **mutual bonds** with their caretakers.

Many of the **preliminary conclusions** about primate language learning were challenged by Herbert Terrace and his **colleagues** in their investigation of Nim. Terrace noticed many subtle characteristics of Nim's communications that seemed **incompatible** with a child's use of language, and he argued that animals in other studies demonstrated these same characteristics.

45 First, Terrace said, the **format** of their sentences was always relatively simple and **brief**. Nim could use **isolated** gestures or could combine two or three gestures, but the chimp never used strings of words or **clauses** that conveyed more sophisticated or **abstract** messages. Second, Terrace **cited** the animals' lack of spontaneity, creativity, and expanding complexity and **adaptation**, which are characteristic of children's language. Many of the animals' sentences were
50 requests for food, tickling, baths, pets, and other pleasurable objects and experiences. Other researchers pointed out that chimps do not **inherently** associate seen objects with heard words, as human infants do. Finally, Terrace questioned whether experimenter bias influenced the reports of the chimps' communications. Consciously or not, experimenters who conclude that chimps learn language might tend to ignore strings that **violate** grammatical order or to
55 reinterpret **ambiguous** strings so that they make grammatical sense. For example, if Nim sees someone holding a banana and signs, "Nim banana," the experimenter might assume the word order is correct and means "Nim wants the banana" rather than "That banana belongs to Nim," in which case the word order would be **inaccurate**.

Linguists and psychologists are still not **unified** about whether our sophisticated mammalian
60 cousins can learn language. Studies are expensive and take many years. Accordingly, the amount of evidence in the area is **minimal**—just a handful of studies, each based on a few animals. **Nevertheless**, two things are clear. First, whatever the chimp, gorilla, and dolphin have learned is a much more primitive and limited form of communication than that learned by children. Second, their level of communication does not do justice to their overall intelligence; these
65 animals are smarter than their "language" production suggests. In **summary**, it is possible to **infer** from the evidence up until now that humans have language abilities that are **unique**, but that under the right circumstances, and with the right tools, other animals can master many language-like skills.

Adapted from Douglas A. Bernstein, Louis A. Penner, Alison Clarke-Stewart, and Edward J. Roy, *Psychology*, 6th ed. (Boston: Houghton Mifflin, 2003), 301–3.

1. VOCABULARY IN CONTEXT

Find the boldface words in each paragraph that correspond to the following meanings.

Paragraph 1	a. _____	continuing
	b. _____	despite
Paragraph 2	c. _____	complicated
	d. _____	adulthood
Paragraph 5	e. _____	a close relationship
	f. _____	tools
Paragraph 6	g. _____	coworkers
	h. _____	initial
	i. _____	dissimilar because of basic differences
Paragraph 7	j. _____	act against a principle
	k. _____	naturally
	l. _____	short
	m. _____	not concrete
	n. _____	having more than one meaning
	o. _____	the process of changing
	p. _____	mentioned as proof
Paragraph 8	q. _____	exceptional, special
	r. _____	very small
	s. _____	nonetheless
	t. _____	deduce

2. READING COMPREHENSION

2A Getting the Facts

1. Put a check mark (✓) next to each species of animal mentioned in the text.

a. _____ gorilla   e. _____ dolphin

b. _____ orangutan   f. _____ bee

c. _____ dog   g. _____ chimpanzee

d. _____ bonobo   h. _____ whale

2. Paragraph 4 describes various studies that test the ability of primates to communicate. Complete the chart to show research information about these primate language studies.

Researchers/ Trainers	Species	Name	Method of Communication
		Sarah	
	pygmy chimpanzee		
Duane Rumbaugh			
			American Sign Language
		Nim Chimsky	

3. Indicate whether the following statements about the information reported in paragraph 5 are true (T) or false (F).

a. _____ The primates could not talk about past events.

b. _____ The vocabulary of the animals focused on concrete objects.

c. _____ The subjects mastered a maximum of 500 words.

d. _____ The primates seemed to be able to communicate about things that were not present.

e. _____ The animals' vocabulary included verbs, nouns, adjectives, and adverbs.

f. _____ The primates could not express wishes.

g. _____ The caretakers and their subjects formed close relationships.

h. _____ Some of the animals did not enjoy the language training sessions.

4. Herbert Terrace and his colleagues concluded that Nim's communications were unlike those of a child. Identify the dissimilar characteristics that they observed. (paragraph 7)

a. _____

b. _____

c. _____

d. _____

e. _____

2B Making Inferences

1. In your own words, what can you conclude from the evidence presented about the linguistic capabilities of primates?

    _____

    _____

2. Why are primates the primary focus of linguists and anthropologists who are researching animal communication?

    _____

    _____

3. Why might some people be against these types of linguistic experiments with animals?

    _____

    _____

> **Keep track of your progress in learning and using new words through self-evaluation and testing.**

3. DICTIONARY SKILLS

Study the dictionary entries for *abstract* and *abstraction*. Then decide whether the sentences below are true (**T**) or false (**F**).

> **ab•stract** (ăb străkt′ *or* ăb′străkt′) *adj.* **1.** Thought of apart from any particular object or thing. For example, *goodness* is an abstract word and *softness* is an abstract quality. **2.** Difficult to understand: *Your complicated explanation is too abstract for me.* **3.** In art, concerned with designs or shapes that do not realistically represent any person or thing: *an abstract painting full of strange shapes.* *-n.* (ăb′străkt′). A brief summary of the main points of a written or spoken text: *an abstract of the President's speech.* *-tr.v.* (ăb străkt′). **1.** To take away or remove (sthg.). **2.** [*from*] To think of (a quality, for example) apart from any particular instance or thing: *abstract a law of nature from a laboratory experiment.* **3.** To make a summary of (sthg.): *It was not easy to abstract his article.* ♦ in the abstract. In theory but not necessarily in reality: *In the abstract, fishing is relaxing, but we found it to be hard work.* **-ab•stract′**ly *adv.* **-ab•stract′**ness *n.* [U]
>
> **ab•strac•tion** (ăb străk′shən) *n.* **1.** [C] An idea or quality thought of apart from any particular instance or thing: *Abstractions are hard to understand.* **2.** [U] Absent-mindedness: *In his abstraction, he didn't say hello.*

1. _____ *Abstract* artists paint pictures of people who look real.

2. _____ The word *abstract* may be a verb, a noun, or an adjective.

3. _____ A person who displays *abstraction* probably has something on his or her mind.

4. _____ Academic journal articles are usually preceded by an *abstract*.

5. _____ The word *table* is an example of an *abstract* noun.

6. _____ The verb *abstract* can be followed by a direct object.

7. _____ An *abstract* idea is more specific than a concrete plan.

8. _____ The word *abstraction* has four syllables.

9. _____ The suffix of *abstraction* shows that the word is a verb.

10. _____ Kindness is an *abstract* quality.

4. WORD FORMS

4A Chart Completion

Complete the following chart with the different forms of each word. Note that some words do not have all forms.

Noun	Verb	Adjective	Adverb
abstract, abstraction	abstract	abstract	abstractedly
		isolated	X
adaptation			X
X	X		inherently
	violate	violated	X
	X	accurate	
		brief	
	cite	cited	X
conclusion			
	X	ambiguous	

4B Word Forms in Sentences

Reread paragraph 7 in the reading selection. Complete a summary of the paragraph with the following words. Make sure that each word fits grammatically and meaningfully.

abstract	adapt	brevity	conclusion	isolated
accuracy	ambiguity	cited	inherent	violations

Terrace challenged the preliminary conclusions about primates' linguistic capacities by first pointing out the (1) _____ of their sentences. Nim only used (2) _____ gestures and did not communicate (3) _____ ideas. Secondly, Terrace (4) _____ their inability to (5) _____ their language to spontaneous situations. Many of the animals' sentences were requests for food and other pleasurable objects and experiences. His colleagues also pointed out that chimpanzees do not have the (6) _____ ability to form associations between seen objects and heard words, as human infants do. Lastly, Terrace questioned whether experimenter bias might have led to the

(7) _____ that chimps can learn language. Perhaps researchers unconsciously ignored (8) _____ of grammar or (9) _____ of meaning by making assumptions about the (10) _____ of word order.

5. COLLOCATIONS

Give **two examples** of each of the following common collocations.

1. traffic violations   _____   _____
2. human rights violations   _____   _____
3. unification of countries   _____   _____
4. family bonds   _____   _____
5. immature behavior   _____   _____
6. explosive devices   _____   _____
7. abstract ideas   _____   _____
8. instruction manuals   _____   _____
9. complex issues   _____   _____
10. unique characteristics of mammals   _____   _____

6. WORD PARTS

-phon-, -ling-, -lang- (sound, hearing)

6A Each of the following words contains the word part -phon-, which means "sound" or "hearing." Write each word next to its meaning.

headphones	microphone	phonograph	symphony
megaphone	phoneme	phonology	telephone

1. _____   The study of sounds in a particular language
2. _____   A device that allows you to speak to another person in a different location
3. _____   An instrument for reproducing sound by means of a needle
4. _____   A long piece of music for an orchestra
5. _____   A cone-shaped device that makes your voice louder
6. _____   A piece of equipment used in recording the voice or making it louder
7. _____   The smallest unit of sound that affects meaning
8. _____   A personal device to put over the ears to listen to music or broadcasts

6B Give a brief definition of the following terms that contain the word part *-ling* or *-lang*, meaning "language."

1. bilingual child   _____

2. native language   _____

3. dead language   _____

4. programming language   _____

5. street language   _____

6. strong language   _____

7. linguistic analysis   _____

8. multilingual class   _____

7. WRITING

7A Writing a Lab Report

You just got a job working as a research assistant with an acknowledged expert in primate language. You are helping to train a chimpanzee to communicate using American Sign Language, and you must write your observations after each session. To prepare for your training sessions, you have already done some research on the Internet about two other primates who learned American Sign Language: Washoe, trained by Beatrice and Allen Gardner, and Nim Chimsky, trained by Herbert Terrace.

Using the following outline as a guide, complete a lab report for your first day of assisting in the observation and language training of the chimpanzee. Try to use at least **six to eight vocabulary words** in your report.

Lab Report   **August 4**

Methods

- Description of subject (age, gender, etc.)
- Description of equipment (audiovisual aids, computer, etc.)
- Description of objectives and procedures

Observations

- Results of learning activities
- Linguistic interactions
- Specific examples

Discussion

- Were the objectives met?
- Were the results similar to previously cited observations?
- What will be the objectives and procedures for the next training session?

7B Paragraph Writing

Write a response to **one** of the following topics. Include at least **six to eight vocabulary words** in your paragraph.

1. Write a paragraph describing your experiences learning a foreign language. What are your strengths and weaknesses in trying to communicate in a different language? How have you dealt with such issues as different writing systems, grammar, and pronunciation? Do you feel confident interacting with native speakers of the language(s) you have learned?

2. Describe an experience you have had listening to young children learning to speak. At what age do they start to speak? What kinds of words do they say first? How do they learn to build sentences, and what kinds of errors in grammar do they tend to make? How do children learn a first language differently from older people who are learning a foreign language?

8. SPEAKING

8A Linguistic Analysis

In the following illustration, the speaker on the right has interpreted the speaker's message in a way that differs from the speaker's intended message. With a partner, analyze the illustration and the message to understand the linguistic confusion between the speaker and the listener. Discuss your experiences of similar linguistic misunderstandings, with specific examples.

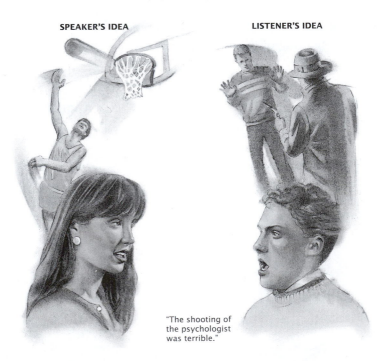

SPEAKER'S IDEA   LISTENER'S IDEA

"The shooting of the psychologist was terrible."

Adapted from Douglas A. Bernstein, Louis A. Penner, Alison Clarke-Stewart, and Edward J. Roy, *Psychology*, 6th ed. (Boston: Houghton Mifflin, 2003), 294.

8B Role-Plays

Using new vocabulary words from this chapter, act out the following role-plays.

1. You are thinking about taking a course in linguistics next semester, but you want to know more about the course before you sign up for it. You visit the linguistics professor during her office hours to find out more about the content of the course, the required assignments, special projects, and the class hours.

2. Your friend just got a job in the primate language training lab at your university. He is very excited to participate in training a chimpanzee to communicate using a computer keyboard. However, you feel that it is unethical to try to humanize animals in this way and to keep them in an artificial environment in the lab. Tell your friend how you feel about his new job and suggest that he find another position that does not exploit wild animals or violate ethical standards.

Address: http://elt.heinle.com/essentialvocab   〉 go

For more activities related to this chapter, go to the *Essential Academic Vocabulary* website.

CHAPTER
15

REVIEW

What do you know about polygraphs (lie detectors)? Test your knowledge by deciding whether the following statements are true (**T**) or false (**F**).

1. _____ A polygraph is a pen and paper test.

2. _____ A polygraph test records specific physical reactions when a person tells a lie.

3. _____ Doctors use polygraphs during medical checkups.

4. _____ Polygraphs are always accurate.

5. _____ Polygraphs may be used to convict criminals in the United States.

6. _____ Some people can manipulate the test to "cheat."

7. _____ Innocent people never have inaccurate results with a polygraph test.

8. _____ There is considerable debate about the usefulness of polygraph tests.

9. _____ A person who fails a polygraph test is automatically considered to be guilty.

10. _____ The word *polygraph* is made up of two word parts that describe the test. *Poly* means "many" and *graph* means "write."

1. VOCABULARY IN CONTEXT

Write the appropriate word from each group of words in the numbered blanks in the text.

1. complex, liberal, virtual
2. fundamental, medical, minimal
3. incompatible, manual, underlying
4. enforced, ignored, revealed
5. device, equipment, infrastructure
6. abstract, dynamic, inherent
7. accuracy, expansion, style
8. brief, isolated, preliminary
9. allocate, expose, substitute
10. ambiguous, neutral, visible
11. bias, devise, devote
12. acknowledge, evolve, violate
13. conclude, display, expand
14. debate, enhance, infer
15. experts, instructors, publishers
16. capable, flexible, incorporated
17. disposing, facilitating, manipulating
18. contacts, conclusions, pursuits
19. debate, maturity, rationalization
20. differentiating, exceeding, sustaining

LIE DETECTION TESTS

Detecting (1) _____ patterns of physical response associated with different emotions is (2) _____ to the lie detection industry. If people experience (3) _____ anxiety or guilt when they tell a lie, specific patterns of physical reactions should be (4) _____ on a piece of (5) _____, called a polygraph, that records heart rate, breathing, skin changes, and other automatic responses.

Most people do have (6) _____ emotional responses when they lie, but statistics about the (7) _____ of polygraphs are difficult to obtain. (8) _____ estimates vary widely, from those suggesting that polygraphs (9) _____ 90 percent of guilty, lying individuals, to those suggesting that polygraphs are (10) _____ in 40 percent of cases. Obviously, the results of a polygraph test are not determined entirely by whether a person is telling the truth. What people think about the act of lying, as well as about the value of the test itself, can also (11) _____ the results. For example, people who consider lying to be acceptable—and who do not (12) _____ the power of polygraphs—are unlikely to (13) _____ emotion-related physiological responses while lying during the test. However, an innocent person who believes in such tests and who thinks that "everything always goes wrong" might show a large fear response when asked about a crime, thus someone might wrongly (14) _____ guilt.

Polygraph tests can detect some liars, but most (15) _____ agree that a guilty person may be (16) _____ of (17) _____ a lie detector. Moreover, inaccurate (18) _____ from the test may lead some innocent people to be mislabeled as guilty. Because of the ongoing (19) _____ about the difficulty of (20) _____ between the guilty and the innocent, a majority of psychologists in the United States do not support the use of polygraph results as evidence in court.

_____

Adapted from Douglas A. Bernstein, Louis A. Penner, Alison Clarke-Stewart, and Edward J. Roy, *Psychology*, 6th ed. (Boston: Houghton Mifflin, 2003), 420–21.

2. SYNONYMS

Match the nouns in column A with their meanings in column B.

Column A		Column B	
1. ____ maturity	8. ____ abstract	**a.** payment	**i.** range
2. ____ conflict	9. ____ incentive	**b.** not supporting either side	**j.** area of knowledge
3. ____ neutrality	10. ____ domain	**c.** idea	**k.** close relationship
4. ____ scope	11. ____ fees	**d.** assumption	**l.** summary
5. ____ expansion	12. ____ bond	**e.** change	**m.** disagreement
6. ____ presumption	13. ____ notion	**f.** behavior of an adult	**n.** increase in size or number
7. ____ transformation	14. ____ clause	**g.** tendency	**o.** motivation
	15. ____ trend	**h.** group of words in a sentence	

3. ODD WORD OUT

Cross out the word in each line that does NOT have a similar meaning to the other three words.

1. instructions, enhancement, directions, orientation
2. nevertheless, nonetheless, virtually, notwithstanding
3. capacity, ability, creativity, capability
4. primarily, ultimately, finally, eventually
5. colleague, coworker, associate, estate
6. transmit, channel, incorporate, convey
7. ongoing, complex, complicated, difficult
8. deduce, dispose, infer, conclude
9. mental, psychological, incompatible, intellectual
10. furthermore, likewise, similarly, correspondingly

4. WORD FORMS IN SENTENCES

Complete the following sentences using the grammatically correct form of the word in italics. (It may be necessary to change a verb form or tense or to make a noun plural.)

1. Although the professor gave _____ directions for the research paper, I was still confused.

    definition, define, definite, definitely

2. The number of words in my term paper _____ the requirement by about 500 words, so I had to shorten it.

    excess, exceed, excessive, excessively

3. The combination of the two chemicals had a _____ effect on them.

    neutrality, neutralize, neutralizing, neutral, neutrally

4. I am currently researching the reasons birds _____ in the winter.

    migration, migrant, migrate

5. There is an _____ of the students' projects in the lab.

    exhibit, exhibition, exhibitionism, exhibito

6. My computer does not have the _____ to download these documents.

    capability, capable, capably

7. When my roommate said that he was working late in the lab, I _____ that he was working on his thesis.

    presumption, presume, presumptive, presumptively

8. In my history course, we are discussing the different ways in which workers were _____ in the early nineteenth century.

    exploitation, exploit, exploitative

9. The article I need for my research paper was _____ in *Psychology Today* in June 1998.

    publication, publisher, publish

10. During the Industrial Revolution, there was a complete _____ of society in urban areas.

    transformation, transformer, transform, transformable

5. COLLOCATIONS

Combine a word from column A with a word in column B to form a common collocation. Then match the two-word collocation with its definition.

Column A		Column B	
traffic	public	contact	lifestyle
mental	medical	rate	arts
seating	virtual	transport	block
survival	alternative	advice	violation
physical	liberal	capacity	reality

1. _____ a temporary inability to remember something

2. _____ vehicles such as trains and buses that you pay a fee to ride

3. _____ a way of living that is different from the norm

4. _____ a rule that is broken by a driver

5. _____ the number of people or animals continuing to live

6. _____ the opinion of a doctor about a health issue

7. _____ the act of touching or being close to another person

8. _____ the maximum number of people allowed in a public space

9. _____ areas of learning that promote abstract thinking and the acquisition of general knowledge

10. _____ a computer environment that simulates real life

6. WORD PARTS

6A Complete the adjectives with the correct ending (-al, -ive, -ent, -ant, -ic, -ish, -ous, -ious, -able).

1. child ____	6. ambigu ____	11. ethn ____	16. fool ____
2. cap ____	7. comfort ____	12. obv ____	17. nerv ____
3. minim ____	8. athlet ____	13. medic ____	18. class ____
4. evid ____	9. baby ____	14. creat ____	19. consider ____
5. medic ____	10. intellig ____	15. virtu ____	20. inher ____

6B Combine the word parts in box A with the word parts in box B to create as many words as possible.

BOX A	BOX B			
micro-	-phone	-eme	-fer	-fuse
tele-	-scribe	-act	-port	-plant
phon-	-mit	-ology	-phony	-etics
mega-	-late	-form	-drama	-path(y)
sym-	-(o)logist	-iatrist		
trans-				
psych(o)-				

microphone, psychodrama _____

_____

_____

_____

_____

Address: `http://elt.heinle.com/essentialvocab` ❯ go

For more activities related to this chapter, go to the *Essential Academic Vocabulary* website.

CHAPTER 16

ENVIRONMENTAL SCIENCE

WORD LIST

Noun	Verb	Adjective	Adverb
controversy	anticipate	adjacent	automatically
couple	complement	coherent	eventually
erosion	confine	comprehensive	inevitably
fluctuation	convert	contemporary	nonetheless
initiative	eliminate	crucial	thereby
ministry	incline	federal	
panel	minimize	forthcoming	
paradigm	offset	integral	
scenario	release	minimum	
sequence	restrain	nuclear	
subsidy	trace	passive	
supplement		persistent	
vehicle		predominant	
		successive	
		uniform	

PREVIEW QUESTIONS

1. What are some differences between renewable and nonrenewable energy sources?

2. What are fossil fuels? What are their advantages and disadvantages?

3. What is meant by alternative energy?

4. In your region, what is the most common form of energy for generating electricity? What is the most common form of energy for heating homes and businesses?

5. What energy sources do people in developing countries use to heat their homes and cook their food?

6. What types of alternative energy sources are used in your region? For what purposes are these energy sources used?

7. If you were going to build a house, what type of alternative energy source would you incorporate into its design? Why?

READING

RENEWABLE ALTERNATIVE ENERGY RESOURCES

1   As the reserves of fossil fuels decrease and environmental damage related to their use **inevitably** increases, governments and industries are seeking alternative ways to **anticipate** growing energy needs. Most existing alternative energy sources are renewable and can be used virtually without depletion or can be replenished over a relatively short period of time. They include geothermal,
5   hydroelectric, tidal, solar, wind energy, and energy produced by burning such renewable organic materials as trees and agricultural waste.

Geothermal Energy
Reykjavik, the capital of Iceland, is relatively pollution free because it has an **adjacent** clean and inexpensive source of energy: Heat from shallow, hot rock beneath the surface is used to **convert**
10   groundwater to hot water and steam. The hot water is circulated through pipes and radiators to heat homes and municipal buildings, and the steam drives electric generators.

Since humans first discovered geothermal heat as an energy source in Larderello, Italy, in 1904, about 20 countries have used it, including the United States. More nations would be **inclined** to take advantage of this relatively inexpensive, nonpolluting energy if they could.
15   Unlike oil, coal, and natural gas, however, geothermal energy cannot be transported, so its use is **confined** to an area close to its source. Every nation using geothermal energy is located on a currently or recently active hot spot.

Hydroelectric Power
For many centuries, humans have used falling water as an energy source to mill flour, saw logs,
20   and power numerous machines. Today, hydroelectric facilities employ falling water to produce electricity. To generate hydroelectric power, a high-volume river is dammed to create enough vertical incline for falling water to **automatically** power the generators.

Hydroelectric power is widely available; since 1983, nearly one-third of all new electricity-generating plants built in the United States have been hydroelectric installations. Furthermore, if
25   every sizable river in the United States were dammed for this purpose, hydroelectric power could supply 50 percent of our total electricity needs. Global hydroelectric development lags even

further behind; only 6 percent of the world's hydroelectric potential is being used, and in South America and Africa, where its potential is greatest, only 1 percent has been developed. At the other extreme, hydroelectric power is **integral** to Canada's economy, with 75 percent of its

30 electricity coming from this clean resource.

Although hydroelectric power is nonpolluting, some **persistent** environmental problems are associated with its use. Dams can disrupt the local ecological balance by altering or destroying wildlife habitat. They may also block natural **erosion** processes—their reservoirs **eventually** fill with sediment that would otherwise replenish coastal beaches. Decisions to build dams must,

35 therefore, balance the environmental costs against the energy yield.

Tidal Power

In coastal areas with a high tidal range—the **fluctuations** in the water surface level between high and low tide—energy from rising and falling water levels can be produced by building a dam across a narrow bay or inlet. The dam's gates are then opened during rising tides and closed to

40 **restrain** the water at its maximum height. During **successive** low tides, the elevated water is channeled seaward to electrical generators, producing renewable, pollution-free energy.

Tidal power production, however, requires a **minimum** tidal range of 8 meters (26 feet), and it disturbs the ecology of surrounding coastal habitats. As yet, no tidal-power facilities in North America have been constructed, although there are a **couple** of strong candidates for future

45 development. Maximum development of the United States' potential tidal power would provide only 1 percent of the nation's total electrical needs, although it could become a significant **supplement** to other energy sources in some areas. Worldwide potential for this energy source, only slightly better, is about 2 percent of the total electricity demand.

Solar Energy

50 Solar-powered pocket calculators and wristwatches take advantage of an energy source that is a **paradigm** of a totally renewable and easily accessible energy source that requires no expensive drilling or destructive strip mining, cannot be monopolized by unfriendly political regimes, and produces no hazardous wastes or air pollution.

Solar heating can be either **passive** or active. Passive solar heating distributes the heat

55 naturally; in northern regions, the simplest way to heat spaces passively is to construct buildings with windows facing south. Sunlight passes through the window glass and heats objects within the room; heat radiates from these objects to warm the air. Such an architectural design, coupled with efficient insulation, **complements** traditional heating systems by sharply reducing both air pollution and the cost of heating with fossil fuels.

60 Active solar heating works via water-filled, roof-mounted **panels** with black linings that absorb maximum sunlight. The solar-heated water is circulated throughout the building for space heating or directly to the building's hot water system. Solar panels are most productive in mild, sunny climates such as Florida, Texas, California, and the Southwest, where they can provide as much as 90 percent of a building's heating needs.

65 ### Wind Power

Wind power is another clean, renewable, nonpolluting energy source whose use for pumping groundwater and powering sawmills and flour mills can be **traced** back over centuries in the Netherlands, where windmills are intrinsic to the rural landscape. Wind power, however, is rarely cost-effective because winds need to blow constantly, forcefully, and from a **uniform** direction

70 for large-scale production.

Biomass

Fuels derived from plants and animals are known collectively as biomass fuels. In developing countries, as much as 35 percent of the energy used for cooking and heating comes from burning two common biomass fuels: wood and animal dung. Biomass fuels also include grain alcohol (an
75 additive to gasoline for **vehicle** use), methane gas **released** from the decaying garbage in landfills, combustible urban trash, and plant waste from crops such as sugarcane, peanuts, and corn. The **predominant** biomass fuel is wood, which heats about 10 percent of **contemporary** North American homes, more than are heated by electricity from **nuclear** power plants.

The advantages of biomass fuel, however, may be **offset** by environmental concerns. Unlike
80 most other renewable resources, biomass fuels can create air pollution and desertification problems when used on a wide scale or implemented poorly. As with oil and coal, burning of this resource introduces poisonous gases and particles into the air, reducing air quality and increasing global warming. Moreover, in arid regions, a common **sequence** of events produces a **scenario** of environmental destruction. An overreliance on cutting down trees for energy leads to the removal
85 of root systems that help retain water and soil, **thereby** contributing to desertification, which consequently **eliminates** animals that provide dung for fuel.

There is considerable **controversy** over the best ways to utilize alternative energy sources. **Federal subsidies** for alternative energy have been **minimized** in recent years, and little support from government **ministries** has been **forthcoming**. **Nonetheless**, it is **crucial** to implement
90 **comprehensive** and **coherent initiatives** to offset energy shortages in the future.

Adapted from Stanley Chernicoff, Haydn A. "Chip" Fox, and Lawrence H. Tanner, *Earth: Geologic Principles and History* (Boston: Houghton Mifflin, 2002), 360–63.

1. VOCABULARY IN CONTEXT

Choose the best meaning according to the context in which the word is used in the reading.

a. inevitably (line 1)	eventually	primarily	unavoidably
b. adjacent (line 8)	near	isolated	overseas
c. convert (line 9)	sustain	transform	devise
d. inclined (line 14)	unifying	likely	sloping
e. confined (line 16)	extracted	exhibited	limited
f. integral (line 29)	visible	incompatible	important
g. persistent (line 31)	dynamic	ongoing	virtual
h. fluctuations (line 37)	changes	capacities	intervals
i. supplement (line 47)	display	presumption	addition
j. paradigm (line 51)	style	model	notion

k. **uniform** (line 69)	constant	alternative	flexible
l. **predominant** (line 77)	marginal	principal	neutral
m. **eliminates** (line 86)	allocates	incorporates	removes
n. **forthcoming** (line 89)	given	modifiable	fundamental
o. **comprehensive** (line 90)	ambiguous	ideological	complete

2. READING COMPREHENSION

2A Getting the Facts

1. In paragraph 1, what two reasons are given for governments and companies to seek alternative energy sources?

   a. _____

   b. _____

2. Six types of alternative energy sources are described in the reading. Complete the following chart to show the characteristics of each source.

Energy Source	Advantages	Disadvantages	Environmental Damage
Geothermal			
Hydroelectric			
Tidal			
Solar			
Wind			
Biomass			

3. Indicate whether the following statements about the information in the reading selection are true (**T**) or false (**F**).

   a. _____ Geothermal heat was discovered in Iceland in 1904.

   b. _____ Africa has developed only 1 percent of hydroelectric potential.

   c. _____ In South America, 75 percent of electricity comes from hydroelectric power.

   d. _____ Worldwide potential for tidal power is estimated to be only 1 percent.

   e. _____ Solar power can provide 90 percent of home heating needs in sunny climates in the United States.

   f. _____ Windmills have been used for centuries in the Netherlands.

   g. _____ Ten percent of homes worldwide use wood for heat.

   h. _____ Biomass fuels consist primarily of methane gas and garbage.

   i. _____ Desertification can occur when too many trees are cut down in dry areas.

   j. _____ Grain alcohol can be added to gasoline used to fuel cars.

2B Making Inferences

1. According to the information provided in the reading and your own general knowledge, list the alternative energy sources in order of widespread use in the United States (*a* being the most widespread, *f* being the least widespread). Be prepared to support your order with evidence from the text, either directly stated or inferred.

biomass	hydroelectric power	tidal power
geothermal energy	solar energy	wind power

   a. _____

   b. _____

   c. _____

   d. _____

   e. _____

   f. _____

2. Why do you think there is controversy over alternative energy sources? Why doesn't the U.S. government provide more financial support for the development of these technologies?

   _____

   _____

   _____

   _____

   _____

> True word knowledge and understanding comes from using words in meaningful situations and activities that require conscious thought and effort.

3. DICTIONARY SKILLS

Study the dictionary entries for *inclination*, *incline*, and *inclined*. Then use a synonym or a short phrase to replace each of the bold words in the following sentences.

> **in•cli•na•tion** (ĭn′klə nā′shən) *n.* **1.** [C; U] A natural tendency to act in a certain way: *Many people have an inclination to sleep late on weekends.* **2.** [U] A slant or slope: *the steep inclination of the roof.*
> **in•cline** (ĭn klīn′) *v.* **in•clined, in•clin•ing, in•clines.** —*intr.* **1.** To slant or slope: *a road that inclines steeply.* **2.** To lower the head or body, as in a nod or bow: *The baby's head inclined on his chest.* —*tr.* **1.** To cause (sthg.) to lean, slant, or slope: *We inclined the boards against the side of the building.* **2.** To cause (sthg.) to bend or bow: *The conductor inclined his head as a signal for us to get ready to play.* —*n.* (ĭn′klīn′). A surface that slants; a slope: *The car skidded down the icy incline of the street.* ♦ **be inclined to.** To be likely: *You might be inclined to change your mind after you read this.*
> **in•clined** (ĭn klīnd′) *adj.* **1.** Sloping, slanting, or leaning: *a ramp inclined at 15 degrees.* **2.** Tending or likely: *a man inclined to act too quickly.*

1. _____ Some people **are inclined** to change their minds about environmental issues after reading scientific reports.

2. _____ In order to generate hydroelectric power, a river must have a dam with a large vertical **incline**.

3. _____ When the old man fell asleep, his head **inclined** on his chest.

4. _____ Mike **inclined** his head to acknowledge that he had seen me.

5. _____ My sister **is inclined** to be impatient with people who are passive.

6. _____ My **inclination** is to keep working on a project without a break until I am finished.

7. _____ I **am inclined** to trust the experts in this case.

8. _____ Behind my house is a wooded **incline** where I cut firewood to heat my house.

9. _____ Although the new energy project is controversial, neither side has shown any **inclination** to discuss it together.

10. _____ I am not mathematically **inclined**, so I tend to avoid courses that involve math.

4. WORD FORMS

4A Chart Completion

Complete the following chart with the different forms of each word. Note that some words do not have all forms.

Noun	Verb	Adjective	Adverb
supplement	*supplement*	*supplementary*	X
	complement		X
		persistent	
subsidy		X	X
	X		inevitably
		coherent	
initiative, initiation			
	uniform	uniform	
			automatically
	X		eventually
		predominant	

4B Word Forms in Sentences

Use the correct form of the word to complete the following sentences. Make sure the word you choose fits meaningfully and grammatically into the sentence.

1. **supplement**   Tidal power could be a _supplementary_ energy source in coastal areas.

2. **complement**   Wood is often used to _____ conventional heating systems in North American homes.

3. **persistent**   Problems from erosion _____ in the environment for decades.

4. **subsidy**   The development of alternative energy was _____ by the government in the past.

5. **inevitably**   There will be _____ shortages of fossil fuels in the future.

6. **coherent**   The environmental report was not _____ written, so it was difficult to understand.

7. **initiative**   Communities can _____ alternative energy projects to compete with fossil fuels.

8. **uniform**   There is little _____ in plans for alternative energy systems for this region.

9. **automatically**   Electricity can be generated by _____ processes.

10. eventually   Dry areas can _____ become deserts if too many trees are cut down.

11. predominant   The _____ of fossil fuel usage in this area has greatly increased air pollution.

5. COLLOCATIONS

The following adjectives are commonly found with specific verbs and adverbs.

Verbs	Adverbs	Adjectives
be, seem, become	remarkably, perfectly, reasonably, very	**coherent**
remain, prove, be, consider something, see something as	absolutely, really, clearly, obviously	**crucial**
be, be situated, lie, stand, be located	directly, immediately	**adjacent**
be	extremely, fully, totally, truly, quite, fairly	**comprehensive**
be	immediately, readily, unusually, not very	**forthcoming**
be	completely, fully, totally, almost, virtually	**automatic**
appear, be, look, seem, become	absolutely, probably, apparently, virtually, politically	**inevitable**
be, prove, become, remain	extremely, highly, somewhat, politically, rather	**controversial**

5A Combine the words from the chart (verb + adverb + adjective) to create meaningful sentences on the topic of alternative energy.

1. _____*The new proposal for the installation of wind power seems <u>remarkably coherent</u>.*_____

2. _____

3. _____

4. _____

5. _____
   _____

6. _____
   _____

7. _____
   _____

8. _____
   _____

5B The following common collocations have specific meanings. Discuss these meanings with a partner or your teacher. Write **five** meaningful sentences that include some of these collocations.

controversial figure	religious conversion
on automatic pilot	school uniform
passive restraints	temperature fluctuations
passive smoking	vehicular homicide
passive vocabulary	worst-case scenario

1. _When I commute to work in my vehicle, I'm on automatic pilot and hardly notice the journey._

2. _____
   _____

3. _____
   _____

4. _____
   _____

5. _____
   _____

6. _____
   _____

6. WORD PARTS

aqua-, -hydr- (water)

Each of the following words contains the Latin word part *aqua-* or the Greek word part *-hydr-*. Both word parts mean "water." In each word notice the word part that gives a clue about the word meaning and the suffix that indicates the part of speech. Match the words with their meanings.

aquaculture	aquarium	aquatic	aqueduct	aquifer
dehydrate	hydroelectricity	hydrophobia	hydroplane	hydrotherapy

1. _____ fear of water

2. _____ remove all the water from food or the body

3. _____ the treatment of disease using water

4. _____ the business of raising fish to sell as food

5. _____ electricity produced by water

6. _____ a structure like a bridge that carries water over a river or valley

7. _____ living or growing in water

8. _____ water under the surface of the earth

9. _____ a plane that can take off from and land on water

10. _____ a glass container or building that houses fish and water animals

7. WRITING

7A Paraphrasing

See *Appendix III* for additional information on paraphrasing.

Rewrite the following sentences in your own words. You can use synonyms, change the grammar structure, and/or change the order of ideas. However, the overall meaning of the sentence should remain the same.

1. As the reserves of fossil fuels decrease and environmental damage related to their use inevitably increases, governments and industries are seeking alternative ways to anticipate the populations' growing energy needs.

    In order to minimize environmental problems and to compensate for the future depletion of oil and coal reserves, countries are looking at alternative energy sources to meet the needs of their people.

2. Maximum development of the United States' potential tidal power would provide only 1 percent of the nation's total electrical needs, although it could become a significant supplement to other energy sources in some areas.

_____

_____

_____

3. Solar power is a paradigm of a totally renewable and easily accessible energy source that requires no expensive drilling or destructive strip mining, cannot be monopolized by unfriendly political regimes, and produces no hazardous wastes or air pollution.

_____

_____

_____

4. Wind power is another clean, renewable, nonpolluting energy source whose use for pumping groundwater and powering sawmills and flour mills can be traced back over centuries in the Netherlands, where windmills are intrinsic to the rural landscape.

_____

_____

_____

5. The predominant biomass fuel is wood, which heats about 10 percent of contemporary North American homes, more than are heated by electricity from nuclear power plants.

_____

_____

_____

6. Unlike most other renewable resources, biomass fuels can create air pollution and desertification problems when used on a wide scale or implemented poorly.

_____

_____

_____

7B Paragraph Writing

Write a response to **one** of the following topics. Include at least **six to eight vocabulary words** in your paragraph.

1. On Assignment: Last semester you took a course on alternative energy and found out from your professor about a volunteer project in Nepal, where you could help rural people build simple, solar-powered stoves for cooking, thereby helping to preserve the land from deforestation. You were immediately interested in this project, signed up, and now find yourself in a remote village in the mountains, far from the comforts of life you are used to.

Write a short letter to a friend describing the village environment, the energy sources used previously by the villagers, and how your solar project will help them.

Dear _____,
Here I am in a small village in Nepal _____
_____
_____
_____
_____
_____
_____
_____
_____

2. Alternative Energy: Write a paragraph explaining which alternative power source would be best to use in the region where you live. What features of the climate or the geography of the area make it the best choice? Do you know of any current use of this power source in your region? What advantages and disadvantages would there be to this power source?

8. SPEAKING

8A Cooperative Learning Research Project

Decide on a specific alternative energy source that all group members wish to learn more about. Each member of the group should search for an interesting article on the Internet about a specific topic related to this energy source. Possible topics for the specific alternative energy source include the following: locations, technology, cost of construction, government subsidies, construction methods, infrastructure, environmental problems, and controversies. Each group member is responsible for reading an article several times and taking notes on the main ideas and supporting details.

Using only brief notes, each group member should give a brief oral summary about the content of the article to the group. Group members should ask questions and discuss issues raised in each article.

Finally, as a group, prepare a short oral summary of the information collected from all the articles to present to the whole class.

8B Partner Discussion: Planning an Energy-Efficient House

You and a partner have just bought some wooded land on a south-facing incline. You plan to build a small house on this property. You want to make sure that your house is environmentally friendly and energy efficient, so you want to rely as little as possible on fossil fuels. Discuss with your partner the location of the house, its design, and ways to incorporate energy-saving features and alternative energy possibilities.

Draw a simple plan of the house, showing some of the crucial design elements. Explain your design to other class members.

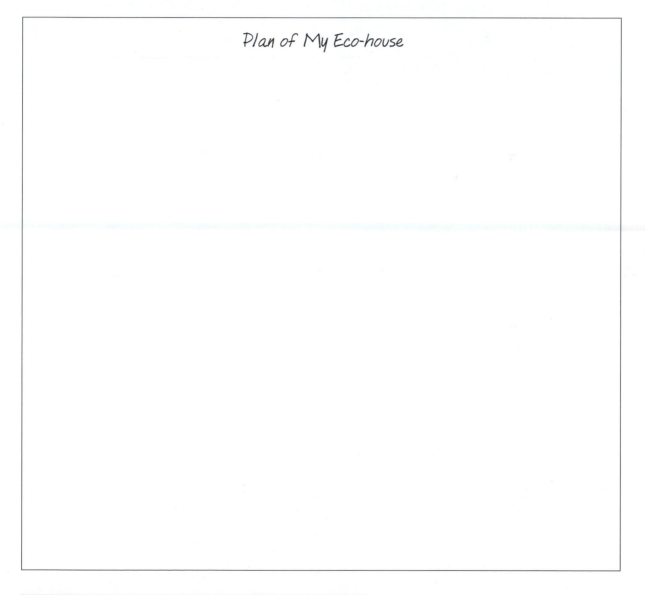

Plan of My Eco-house

For more activities related to this chapter, go to the *Essential Academic Vocabulary* website.

CHAPTER 17

GEOLOGY

WORD LIST

Noun	Verb	Adjective	Conjunction
collapse	accumulate	dramatic	whereby
duration	attain	empirical	
layer	clarify	enormous	
phenomenon	coincide	logical	
version	conceive	reverse	
	confirm	so-called	
	conform	sole	
	diminish	widespread	
	displace		
	find		
	inhibit		
	invoke		
	overlap		
	precede		
	revise		
	trigger		

PREVIEW QUESTIONS

1. What is the connection between dinosaurs and geologists?

2. Have you ever seen reconstructions or models of dinosaurs in museums? What was your impression?

3. What do you think caused the extinction of the dinosaurs?

4. What movies have you seen about dinosaurs? How were the dinosaurs represented?

5. There are many children's books and a lot of media attention given to dinosaurs. Why do you think people are so interested in dinosaurs?

6. What other life forms disappeared at the same time as the dinosaurs?

7. Where in the world have dinosaur fossils been found?

READING

WHAT CAUSED THE EXTINCTION OF THE DINOSAURS?

1   Paleontologists (geologists who study the fossils of ancient life forms) have long wondered what might have caused the **phenomenon** of mass extinction, **whereby** more than 75 percent of all the life forms then on Earth vanished about 65 million years ago. The most **dramatic** loss involved the extinction of the dinosaurs, a group of animals that had roamed the planet for
5   150 million years. Numerous other life forms vanished as well—large and small, water and land dwelling, plant and animal. Many species, whether living in freshwater lakes, in rivers, in saltwater oceans, or on land, became extinct at roughly the same time.

Some early hypotheses focused on a **sole** organism to explain these extinctions. Some hypotheses proposed that epidemic diseases **triggered** the elimination of dinosaur populations or
10   that egg-stealing mammals destroyed dinosaur nests. But neither of these hypotheses **conformed** to the fact that two-thirds of all marine animal species were also lost, which led some scientists to propose that the oceans became lethally salty (though this idea did not explain why some marine creatures survived). To explain the extinction of **enormous** terrestrial reptiles, tiny marine organisms, and many life forms in between, a number of hypotheses **invoked** global
15   environmental change. Did Earth suffer from a period of drastic cooling 65 million years ago? Did a shift in the planet's protective magnetic field allow harmful solar radiation to reach land and sea, eliminating a wide variety of life forms? Did a nearby star explode, bathing Earth in cosmic radiation? Surely, each of these events would have affected all life on Earth simultaneously. Why, then, did 25 percent of the planet's species remain unaffected?

20   Several hypotheses agree that some catastrophic **collapse** of the global food chain **preceded widespread** extinction. One group of scientists has proposed that massive volcanic eruptions on India's Deccan plateau may have been such an event. The rocks of these eruptions have been dated to 65 million years ago, **coinciding** perfectly with the extinction of the dinosaurs. It is postulated that the eruptions sent a cloud of volcanic ash and gas around Earth, blocking out sunlight,
25   cooling the planet, and **diminishing** vegetation, including microscopic plants. Without the plants on which their diets were based, many plant-eating animals would have died, and their extinction would in turn have **displaced** the meat-eaters, such as *Tyrannosaurus rex*, that ate them.

Another group of scientists, led by geologist Walter Alvarez and his father, Nobel Prize–winning physicist Luis Alvarez, **conceived** another scenario: A meteorite at least 10

30 kilometers (6 miles) in diameter plowed into Earth, releasing a shower of pulverized rock into the atmosphere. The resulting dust veil would have blocked out sunlight (in much the same way volcanic ash would have), cooled the planet, and led to a **so-called** "impact winter" with a possible **duration** of decades—long enough to destroy the global food chain. The strongest **empirical** evidence to support this impact hypothesis is a 2-centimeter- (1-inch) thick **layer** of

35 clay found around the world in rocks that date from approximately 65 million years ago. The clay contains iridium, an element that is extremely rare in rocks of terrestrial origin but is quite common in meteorites. Mineral grains shattered by very high pressures—as would occur if a meteorite had struck them—have also been found at the proposed impact sites. The Alvarezes and their associates make the **logical** claim that the iridium-rich layer resulted from the

40 widespread fallout of meteorite dust. Fossils of numerous species, including many now-extinct organisms, had **accumulated** in the rocks that formed just before the iridium-rich layer was deposited, whereas only about one-fourth as many species are **found** in the rocks formed just after this layer was deposited. This evidence suggests that numerous extinctions occurred during the time of deposition.

45 Just as hypotheses may be discarded, **revised,** or **confirmed** and elevated to theory status, they also sometimes **overlap**. One group of scientists has recently proposed that Earth was indeed struck by a meteorite 65 million years ago somewhere in the Western Hemisphere, and that the impact initiated massive volcanism on the **reverse** side of the globe. The material thrown into the atmosphere by both events may have combined to **inhibit** the growth of vegetation,

50 thus eventually bringing about the death of the dinosaurs.

As yet, no **version** of the extinction hypothesis has **attained** theory status. Analysis of these 65-million-year-old deposits continues today, as scientists seek to **clarify** the proportions of organisms that became extinct at that time and search for additional evidence of a meteorite strike or of a catastrophic volcanic eruption that coincides with the time of the extinctions.

Adapted from Stanley Chernicoff, Haydn A. "Chip" Fox, and Lawrence H. Tanner, *Earth: Geologic Principles and History* (Boston: Houghton Mifflin, 2002), 4–5.

1. VOCABULARY IN CONTEXT

Determine how the boldface words are used in the reading. Then for each item, choose the word or phrase that is closest in meaning.

1. _____ **phenomenon** (line 2)
   a. controversy
   b. peculiarity
   c. sequence

2. _____ **sole** (line 8)
   a. single
   b. coherent
   c. uniform

3. _____ **preceded** (line 20)
   a. predicted
   b. predominated
   a. predated

4. _____ **diminishing** (line 25)
   a. reducing
   b. inclining
   c. producing

5. _____ **displaced** (line 27)
   a. traced
   b. eliminated
   c. complemented

6. _____ **empirical** (line 34)
   a. integral
   b. crucial
   c. observed

7. _____ **accumulated** (line 41)
   a. gathered
   b. eliminated
   c. released

8. _____ **confirmed** (line 45)
   a. confined
   b. validated
   c. converted

9. _____ **inhibit** (line 49)
   a. persist
   b. propose
   c. prevent

10. _____ **attained** (line 51)
   a. initiated
   b. reached
   c. supplemented

2. READING COMPREHENSION

2A Getting the Facts

1. What do paleontologists study?

   _____

2. How long ago was the mass extinction of 75 percent of all life forms on Earth?

   _____

3. What kinds of animals became extinct at this time?

   _____

   _____

4. Put a check mark (✓) next to each hypothesis of mass extinction that is mentioned in the second paragraph of the reading.

   a. _____ A single organism was responsible.

   b. _____ Earth was flooded for a long period of time.

   c. _____ Epidemic diseases killed the dinosaurs.

   d. _____ Animals stole the eggs from dinosaur nests.

   e. _____ The largest dinosaurs ate all the smaller ones.

   f. _____ The oceans became too salty to support life.

   g. _____ Earth became much colder for a period of time.

   h. _____ Earth became a desert.

   i. _____ Radiation from the sun killed many species.

   j. _____ The climate became too hot to support life.

   k. _____ Radiation from the explosion of a star killed many life forms.

5. What is wrong with the hypotheses mentioned in the second paragraph?

   _____

   _____

   _____

6. One group of scientists has proposed that volcanic eruptions in India may have caused the extinctions. Put the following events from the third paragraph in the correct sequence, numbering them from 1 to 7, according to this hypothesis.

   _____ blanketing of Earth with volcanic ash and gas

   _____ cooling of the planet   _____ blocking out of sunlight

   _____ massive volcanic eruptions   _____ elimination of meat-eating animals

   _____ death of vegetarian animals   _____ great reduction of plant life

7. The Alvarezes proposed the hypothesis that a meteorite was responsible for the mass extinction. In your own words, summarize the empirical evidence they have discovered to support this hypothesis.

   _____

   _____

   _____

8. Explain the recent hypothesis proposed by a group of scientists that combines two previous hypotheses.

   _____

   _____

   _____

2B Making Inferences

1. What is meant by an impact winter? (paragraph 4)

   _____

   _____

2. Why have there been so many conflicting hypotheses about the extinctions of dinosaurs and other life forms?

   _____

   _____

> The effort involved in trying to remember a word helps you to learn it.

3. DICTIONARY SKILLS

Study the dictionary entries for *confirm*, *confirmation*, and *confirmed*. Complete each sentence with an appropriate ending from the following choices. Write the letter of the choice on the blank.

con•firm (kən fûrm′) *tr.v.* **1.** To support or establish the truth or validity of (sthg.): *The results of the experiment confirmed the theory.* **2.** To make (sthg.) firmer; strengthen: *Reading about famous scientists confirmed her plan to study chemistry.* **3.** To make (sthg.) valid or binding by a formal or legal act: *The judge's appointment to the Supreme Court was confirmed by the Senate.* **4.** To admit (sbdy.) to full membership in a church by confirmation: *Their 13-year-old was confirmed last weekend.*
con•fir•ma•tion (kŏn′fər ma′shən) *n.* [C; U] **1.** The act of confirming: *The President needs the Senate's confirmation to appoint an ambassador.* **2.** Something that confirms; proof: *The driver's license was confirmation of the man's age.* **3.** A religious ceremony that allows sbdy. to be a full member of a church: *We held a reception to celebrate our son's confirmation.*
con•firmed (kən fûrmd′) *adj.* **1.** Firmly established; proved: *a confirmed theory.* **2.** Settled in a habit or condition: *a confirmed gossip.*

   a. of their identity

   b. Dr. Jenkins had to leave the paleontology conference early

   c. the hypothesis

   d. as an extinction theory

   e. as the chairperson of the Geology Department

   f. so he always takes vacations in places where he can search for fossils

   g. her intention to be a geologist

   h. that dinosaurs existed in this area long ago

1. The newly found fossils provided **confirmation** _h_.
2. The analysis of the data **confirmed** ____.
3. Visiting the Grand Canyon as a child **confirmed** ____.
4. A family party celebrated Dr. Smithton's **confirmation** ____.
5. In order to attend her son's **confirmation**, ____.
6. My father is a **confirmed** fossil hunter, ____.
7. Paleontologists have to show identification in some countries as **confirmation** ____.
8. No extinction hypothesis has yet been **confirmed** ____.

4. WORD FORMS

4A Chart Completion

Complete the chart with the corresponding noun form of each verb.

Verb	Noun
accumulate	accumulation
inhibit	
attain	
clarify	
coincide	
diminish	
displace	
invoke	
reverse	
collapse	
dramatize	
trigger	
precede	

4B Word Forms in Sentences

Create **five** new sentences about the mass extinction of dinosaurs, using a noun and a verb from the chart in the previous exercise in each sentence.

1. _____ The _collapse_ of the dinosaurs may have been _triggered_ by a meteorite. _____
2. _____
3. _____
4. _____
5. _____
6. _____

5. COLLOCATIONS

5A The following verbs are typically found in combination with specific nouns. Match the verbs with the nouns to make meaningful phrases.

accumulate	conceive	dramatize	reverse
attain	confirm	inhibit	trigger

1. _____ a disaster   4. _____ independence   7. _____ a decision
2. _____ identity   5. _____ wealth   8. _____ a child
3. _____ growth   6. _____ a story

5B In each of the following sentences, add an adverb that commonly collocates with the boldface verb. The adverb should reflect the content of the reading.

completely	fully	rapidly	significantly	sufficiently
easily	further	roughly	slightly	totally
exactly	partially	seriously	steadily	virtually

1. This hypothesis seems to **conform** _____ to the facts.
2. Several hypotheses agree that the food chain **collapsed** _____ prior to the extinctions.
3. Knowledge about dinosaurs has **accumulated** _____ in the last few years.
4. Hypotheses cannot be **confirmed** _____.
5. Atmospheric dust _____ **inhibited** the growth of vegetation.

6. No extinction hypothesis has _____ **attained** the status of theory.

7. A meteorite strike might have _____ **coincided** with a volcanic eruption.

8. Sometimes hypotheses are _____ **reversed**.

9. Opinions of scientists tend to **overlap** _____.

10. The mass extinction hypothesis may be _____ **clarified** in the future.

6. WORD PARTS

over- (higher, greater, too much)

The prefix *over-* means "higher," "greater," or "too much."

Verbs	Adjectives
overcharge	overcrowded
overdo	overdressed
overdose	overdue
overeat	overexcited
overflow	overjoyed
overhear	overlong
overpay	overnight
overreact	overpopulated
oversleep	overpriced
overspend	overqualified
overturn	overseas
overwork	overweight

Complete each sentence with a verb or an adjective that summarizes the meaning of the sentence. Be sure to use the correct tense of the verbs.

1. Jim didn't wake up until 9:00, so he missed the meeting. He __*overslept*__.

2. This coat costs far too much. It's __*overpriced*__.

3. My sister has put on about 30 pounds in the last year. She's _____

4. Bill took too much medicine and had to go to the hospital. He _____.

5. I went to see the new movie, but it lasted three hours. It was _____.

6. I don't know why Elizabeth was so angry when she heard the news. She _____.

7. My sister gave birth to a baby girl last night. I'm _____.

8. I paid $25 for this shirt, but it was supposed to cost only $20. I was _____.

9. My father has a job in Europe at the moment. He's _____.

10. Ben wore his best suit to the party, but he should have worn jeans. He was _____.

11. I ate a whole pizza for lunch, and now I feel sick. I _____.

12. I didn't get the job because they're looking for someone with only an undergraduate degree. I was _____.

13. It rained so hard that the water from the river almost reached our house. The river _____.

14. He was supposed to arrive at 5:00, but now it's 7:00. He's _____.

15. This area used to be quiet and uncrowded, but now there are people and cars everywhere. It's _____.

7. WRITING

7A Writing a Summary

See *Appendix IV* for additional information on summarizing.

Reread the article "What Caused the Extinction of the Dinosaurs?" OR find another article on the Internet about the mass extinction of the dinosaurs. Take notes in your own words about the main ideas and supporting details in the text. Use your notes to summarize the article. Include and underline at least **six to eight vocabulary words** in your summary.

7B Paragraph Writing

Write a response to **one** of the following topics. Include at least **six to eight vocabulary words** in your paragraph.

1. There have been several popular movies about dinosaurs in the last few years, including *The Lost World*, *Jurassic Park*, and *Dinosaur Island*. There have also been many video and computer games featuring dinosaurs. Write a paragraph describing one dinosaur movie that you have seen or one game that you have played. Focus on the special effects used and how the main characters interacted with the dinosaurs. Do you think that the dinosaurs were depicted realistically? Were the dinosaurs frightening? What was your overall impression of the movie or game?

2. In most areas of the world, there are interesting geological features that show how the land has changed over time. Describe an interesting geological formation near your university or in a place you have visited. What other geological features are visible in this region? What do these features reveal about how the land has changed? Are there any fossils in this area? What surprises or interests you about these formations?

8. SPEAKING

8A Partner Activity: Researching a Geological Formation

With a partner, research a place with interesting geological formations or fossil remains. Many U.S. national parks and monuments, along with other geological features in the United States and the world, have many geological features. Here are a few places to get you started:

- Grand Canyon National Park, Arizona
- Badlands National Park, South Dakota
- Canyonlands National Park, Utah
- Dinosaur National Monument, Utah and Colorado
- Carlsbad Caverns National Park, New Mexico
- Arches National Park, Utah
- Petrified Forest National Park, Arizona
- the San Andreas Fault, California
- Mt. Fuji, Japan
- the Great Rift Valley, Africa

Your research should focus on the geology of the area, any fossil discoveries, and any hypotheses or theories associated with the formations.

Prepare with your partner a short oral presentation with visuals (photographs, illustrations, and maps) to show the class.

8B Role-Plays

Using new vocabulary words from this chapter, act out the following role-plays.

1. You are planning a trip with a friend to the American West this summer. You want to hike down to the bottom of the Grand Canyon to see all the layers of rock exposed through erosion. However, your friend wants to go to Dinosaur National Monument to see the collections of dinosaur bones that are displayed there. Discuss the trip with your friend and try to make a decision about which place to visit.

2. You are taking a geology class this semester, and your professor has just given a lecture about the mass extinction of the dinosaurs and the various hypotheses that scientists have proposed. Afterward, you debate with a friend which hypothesis seems the most likely. You think a meteorite was the cause, but your friend thinks it was a massive volcanic eruption. Use examples to support your opinion.

Address: http://elt.heinle.com/essentialvocab   ▸ go

For more activities related to this chapter, go to the *Essential Academic Vocabulary* website.

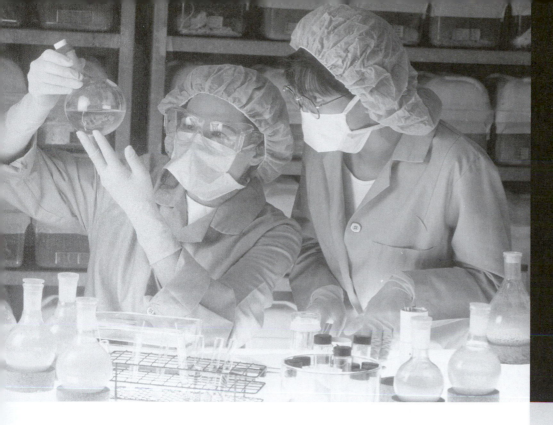

CHEMISTRY

WORD LIST

Noun	Verb		Adjective	Conjunction
aggregate	assemble	quote	external	albeit
author	attach	reject	infinite	
bulk	confer	submit	intense	
foundation	encounter	suspend	odd	
guideline	feature	terminate	visual	
insertion	guarantee			
paragraph	highlight			
portion	implicate			
practitioner	induce			
prospect	inspect			
recovery	proceed			

PREVIEW QUESTIONS

1. Have you ever taken a chemistry course? What are the specific challenges of chemistry courses?

2. How does chemistry affect our lives on a daily basis? What kinds of chemical reactions are useful to us?

3. How does chemistry affect what we eat?

4. What advances in medicine are possible because of chemistry?

5. What might be some disadvantages of using chemicals? Do you know of any chemical reactions that are dangerous or any side effects from the manufacture or use of chemicals?

6. What kinds of jobs are available for chemistry majors? Do you think there is a high demand for people with chemistry degrees?

READING

CHEMISTRY FACTS: THE GOOD, THE BAD, AND THE *ODD*

1 *All changes we produce consist in separating particles that are in a state of cohesion or combination, and joining those that were previously at a distance.*

John Dalton (1766–1844)

Our environment is composed of atoms and molecules that undergo chemical changes to
5   produce the many substances we need and use. In producing new products, energy is released or absorbed. The following **paragraphs** explain some of the **infinite** number of ways we use chemistry in our daily lives. Some of these ways are beneficial to our lives; others may be harmful or dangerous. Still other paragraphs describe chemical reactions that we may consider **odd**.

   a. Heat packs called glove warmers contain powdered iron (and other components) moistened
10   with a little water. When the plastic cover is removed, air can penetrate the paper packet, producing the rusting of iron. This effect on the large surface area of the iron particles causes the "rusting" reaction to **proceed** fast enough to generate a comfortable amount of heat.

   b. Air containing as little as 1.5 parts of carbon monoxide to 100 parts of air may be fatal if breathed for some time. Each year more than 200 people in the United States are killed by
15   carbon monoxide poisoning in the home. Carbon monoxide has no odor, color, or taste. People are most at risk when asleep, so new housing **guidelines** recommend installing several detectors and regularly **inspecting** appliances that burn fossil fuels.

   c. The name *phosphorus* means "light-bearing" and refers to the glowing of "white" phosphorus when it **encounters** oxygen. A reference to white phosphorus can be found in a Sherlock
20   Holmes mystery, wherein a large dog is coated with white phosphorus to scare someone to death.

   d. The **insertion** of bleach into a toilet bowl with other cleaners or ammonia-based cleaners releases chlorine gas, which can have a deadly effect.

   e. Dinitrogen oxide, also known as laughing gas, was discovered by Joseph Priestly and was the
25   first general anesthetic. Dinitrogen oxide is extremely soluble in whipping cream, so it is used as the propellant to produce **portions** of "instant" whipping cream from a spray can.

   f. In 1947 a ship carrying ammonium nitrate exploded in the harbor of Texas City, Texas, killing 576 people. The same chemical was **implicated** in the explosions in the World Trade

Center in New York City in 1993 and the federal office building in Oklahoma City in 1995.
30   Farmers buy ammonium nitrate in **bulk** for use as a fertilizer.

g. Seawater is 2.7 percent salt, but the concentration of salt in the Dead Sea is a huge 27 percent. This extreme saltiness helps to **suspend** people in the water as they bathe for medical reasons.

h. The yellow-brown color of the poisonous photochemical smog that is most **intense** over large cities is due to nitrogen dioxide that forms in the atmosphere from the emissions of vehicle
35   engines.

i. In 1855, pure aluminum sold for $100,000 a pound and was **featured** in an exhibition with the crown jewels of France. Charles Martin Hall was a student at Oberlin College when his chemistry professor remarked that anyone who found an inexpensive way to manufacture aluminum would be **guaranteed** to make a fortune. This remark **induced** Hall to **assemble**
40   the first aluminum made from galvanic cells from fruit jars in 1886. By 1890 aluminum sold for $2 a pound. Hall **conferred** $3 million to Oberlin College when he died.

j. In 2001 medical **practitioners** encouraged parents to **reject** mercury-containing thermometers and to purchase digital thermometers instead. The amount of mercury in a single thermometer, if ingested, is generally not enough to cause harm. However, if the
45   thermometer breaks and the mercury vaporizes, the inhaled mercury can contribute significant problems to a child's neurological development.

k. Skywriting results when an airplane sprays titanium chloride into the air. It reacts with moisture in the air to form titanium dioxide, a compound that constitutes the white **visual** effect of "writing" we see in the sky.

50 l. Every year about 21,000 small children undergo emergency procedures in the United States after putting coins (primarily pennies) into their mouths or noses. Apart from the **prospect** of choking, pennies made after 1981 are not made of 95 percent copper, but of 98 percent zinc, **albeit** with a copper coating. The zinc in these newer pennies can react with the stomach's hydrochloric acid to produce a toxic **aggregate**.

55 m. The active ingredients present in fire retardants dropped from planes onto forest fires are ammonium sulfate and ammonium phosphate. After the fire has **terminated**, the compounds act as fertilizer to aid in the **recovery** of forest growth.

n. On hot days, dedicated fishers select deep areas for fishing. Deep areas are cooler, and more oxygen is dissolved in cooler water than in warmer water near the surface. Fish will naturally
60   congregate in areas with more dissolved oxygen.

o. In July 2001 a *Time* magazine article stated that 98 percent of the wood sold for **external** use in the United States is treated with chromated copper or arsenate. The article's **author**, Jeffrey Kluger, **quoted** research describing the use of arsenic in the assembly of picnic tables, decks, and children's play equipment. Investigators who tested soil in Florida's playgrounds **submitted**
65   reports that **highlighted** arsenic levels far higher than hazardous waste experts consider safe.

p. The **foundation** of a pearl is a grain of sand that has entered the shell of an oyster. Layers of calcium carbonate **attach** themselves around the sand to create a pearl. Pearls generally take about three years or more to form in this way.

Adapted from James T. Shipman, Jerry D. Wilson, and Aaron W. Todd, *An Introduction to Physical Science*, 10th ed. (Boston: Houghton Mifflin, 2003), 310–11, 328–29.

1. VOCABULARY IN CONTEXT

Determine how the words in column A are used in the reading. Then choose the word or phrase in column B that is closest in meaning.

	Column A		**Column B**
1. _____	proceed (line 12)	**a.**	gave
2. _____	encounters (line 19)	**b.**	move
3. _____	insertion (line 22)	**c.**	emphasized
4. _____	bulk (line 30)	**d.**	throw away
5. _____	suspend (line 32)	**e.**	basis
6. _____	induced (line 39)	**f.**	meets
7. _____	assemble (line 39)	**g.**	though
8. _____	conferred (line 41)	**h.**	large quantity
9. _____	reject (line 42)	**i.**	mixture
10. _____	prospect (line 51)	**j.**	keep afloat
11. _____	albeit (line 53)	**k.**	convinced
12. _____	aggregate (line 54)	**l.**	produce
13. _____	recovery (line 57)	**m.**	restoration
14. _____	highlighted (line 65)	**n.**	introduction
15. _____	foundation (line 66)	**o.**	possibility

2. READING COMPREHENSION

2A Getting the Facts

1. Determine whether the following statements about the chemistry facts in the reading are true (**T**) or false (**F**).

   a. _____ The rusting of iron produces heat.

   b. _____ Carbon monoxide can be tasted, smelled, and seen.

   c. _____ Phosphorus has a white glow when it is mixed with oxygen.

   d. _____ Bleach is always a safe household cleaner.

   e. _____ Laughing gas is used in spray cans of whipping cream.

   f. _____ Ammonium nitrate is both a fertilizer and an explosive.

   g. _____ The Dead Sea is so salty that people can float in it.

h. _____ Smog is formed from the nitrogen dioxide in vehicle emissions.

i. _____ Aluminum was cheap to produce in 1855.

j. _____ Thermometers containing mercury are safer than digital thermometers.

k. _____ Skywriting is a visual chemical effect.

l. _____ Copper pennies may be harmful to the health if swallowed.

m. _____ The fire retardants dropped from planes onto forest fires prohibit the regrowth of trees.

n. _____ Fish like to swim in deep water where there is less oxygen.

o. _____ Arsenic is a poisonous substance that is often used to preserve wood for outside use.

p. _____ Pearls are formed when an insect inside an oyster shell is covered by layers of calcium carbonate.

2. The title of the reading is "Chemistry Facts: The Good, the Bad, and the *Odd*." Read the chemistry facts in exercise 1 and give each one an appropriate label: **G** (good), **B** (bad), or **O** (odd). Compare your labels with a partner's labels and be prepared to support your selections.

a. _____	**e.** _____	**i.** _____	**m.** _____
b. _____	**f.** _____	**j.** _____	**n.** _____
c. _____	**g.** _____	**k.** _____	**o.** _____
d. _____	**h.** _____	**l.** _____	**p.** _____

3. Scan the reading to match the chemicals with the common products or uses mentioned.

a. _____ nitrogen dioxide   **1.** skywriting

b. _____ ammonium sulfate/phosphate   **2.** thermometers

c. _____ zinc   **3.** forest fires

d. _____ titanium dioxide   **4.** pearls

e. _____ mercury   **5.** household cleaners

f. _____ iron particles   **6.** smog

g. _____ carbon monoxide   **7.** general anesthetic

h. _____ chlorine gas   **8.** outdoor furniture

i. _____ dinitrogen oxide   **9.** fertilizer

j. _____ ammonium nitrate   **10.** pennies

k. _____ arsenate   **11.** heating equipment

l. _____ calcium carbonate   **12.** heat packs

2B Making Inferences

1. In your own words, what is the meaning of the quotation by John Dalton at the beginning of the reading?

   _____

   _____

   _____

2. Some of the chemical reactions described in the reading may be harmful to your health. Why do you think harmful chemicals are available to the public? Should chemical companies and manufacturers be held responsible in case of injuries or death from these chemicals?

   _____

   _____

   _____

   _____

> You must pay close attention to a word to learn it most effectively.

3. Dictionary Skills

Review the dictionary entries for *odd, oddity,* and *odds*. Complete the following sentences by filling in the blanks with an appropriate word.

odd (ŏd) *adj.* **1.** Unusual; peculiar; strange: *odd behavior; an odd name.* **2.** Being one of an incomplete set or pair: *an odd shoe.* **3.** Not regular or expected: *The client telephoned at odd intervals.* **4.** Relating to whole numbers that are not divisible by two: *Three, five, and seven are odd numbers.* **5.** *(used with even numbers).* More than the number indicated: *There were 20-odd guests at the party.* ♦ **oddball.** *Informal.* A strange person: *He is something of an oddball.* **odd job.** A temporary job that doesn't require skill or training: *She worked at a series of odd jobs during college.* **odd man out.** A person not included in a group: *Without a date, I felt like the odd man out at the party.* —**odd′ly** *adv.* —**odd′ness** *n.* [U]

odd•i•ty (ŏd′ĭ tē) *n., pl.* **odd•i•ties. 1.** [C] A person or thing that is strange: *The three-legged cat was an oddity.* **2.** [U] The condition of being odd; strangeness: *The oddity of his behavior worried me.*

odds (ŏdz) *pl.n.* **1.** The likelihood or probability that sthg. will happen: *The odds are that it will rain tomorrow.* **2.** The chances for and against a certain event: *odds of 20 to 1.* ♦ **at odds.** In disagreement; in conflict: *They were at odds about what to do with the money.* **odds and ends.** Small items of various kinds: *a drawer filled with odds and ends.* **odds are.** It is likely: *The odds are that he'll fail the test.*

1. My brother likes to do chemistry experiments with _____ he finds around the house.

2. When I was a teenager, I did _____ jobs to make some money.

3. White deer are an _____, but you can see them once in a while.

4. There were 50-_____ people at the chemistry meeting.

5. It's _____ that the professor didn't show up for class.

6. My brother was so tall in elementary school that he always felt like the _____.

7. This chemical has a very _____ name.

8. Professor Branston is something of an _____, but he's always willing to help students.

9. The _____ are that the chemistry test tomorrow will be really hard.

10. I was _____ with my partner about which lab experiment to do first.

11. Dr. Lee told us to do the assignments from the _____ pages in the textbook.

12. I couldn't find two matching socks, so I had to wear two _____ ones.

4. WORD FORMS IN SENTENCES

Complete the sentences using the grammatically correct form of the word in italics.

1. There are an _____ number of chemical reactions in the natural world.
   infinity, infinite, infinitely

2. The sea looked _____ blue from the reflection of the blue sky above.
   intensity, intensify, intense, intensely

3. It is difficult for students to _____ what they will be doing 20 years from now.
   visualization, visualize, visual, visually

4. Please e-mail me your résumé in an _____.
   attachment, attach, attachable

5. Home heating appliances should undergo a yearly _____ to eliminate the risk of carbon monoxide poisoning.
   inspector, inspection, inspect, inspected

6. This equipment is so _____ that I need to get some help to move it.
   bulk, bulky, bulkily

7. There is an orientation tomorrow for _____ chemistry majors.
   prospect, prospect, prospective

8. It can take a long time to make a full _____ from the effects of carbon monoxide poisioning.
    recovery, recover, recoverable

9. This experiment requires your full attention, so you should _____ carefully.
    procedure, proceed, procedural

10. Professor Jamison says the oddest things; she's very _____!
    quotation, quote, quotable

5. COLLOCATIONS

5A In the space provided, write the word that can precede all four words in each group to form common collocations.

confer	highlight	implicate	insert	purchase

1. _____*confer*_____ a degree, an award, a prize, a medal
2. _____ criminals, suspects, thieves, wrongdoing
3. _____ the importance, differences, similarities, achievements
4. _____ a house, a car, a television, food
5. _____ money, coins, a credit card, disk

inspect	quote	submit	terminate	undergo

6. _____ manuscripts, articles, budgets, assignments
7. _____ employment, peace talks, weapons tests, pregnancy
8. _____ surgery, change, a bad experience, a transformation
9. _____ luggage, bags, passports, visas
10. _____ a study, an author, a poet, a writer

5B Using the collocations from exercise A, create **ten** sentences that clearly illustrate the meanings of the collocations.

1. _____Undergraduate degrees and special awards were conferred at the graduation ceremony last week._____

2. _____
   _____

3. _____
   _____

4. _____
   _____

5. _____
   _____

6. _____
   _____

7. _____
   _____

8. _____
   _____

9. _____
   _____

10. _____
    _____

11. _____
    _____

6. WORD PARTS

Verb Suffixes: -ate, -ify, -ize, -en

6A The suffixes in the chart are common verb endings that all mean "make," "become," or "have." Add three verbs to each row in the chart.

Verb Suffixes	Examples
-ate	graduate, concentrate, create,
-ify	clarify, falsify, unify,
-ize	minimize, legalize, authorize,
-en	thicken, lighten, harden,

6B Give the correct verb forms, with the appropriate suffix, of the following nouns.

1. implication _____
2. termination _____
3. intensity _____
4. visualization _____
5. fluctuation _____
6. initiative _____
7. subsidy _____
8. elimination _____
9. maximum _____
10. integration _____

11. passivity _____
12. fright _____
13. accumulation _____
14. drama _____
15. administration _____
16. strength _____
17. organization _____
18. regulation _____
19. simplification _____
20. memorization _____

7. WRITING

7A Biography of Antoine Lavoisier

Antoine Lavoisier is commonly called the father of modern chemistry. Write a short biography of Lavoisier in paragraph format, highlighting the principal events of his life. Use connectors (for example, *first, in addition, afterward, then*) and adverbial clauses (for example, *after, before, while*) to combine the facts in a logical and coherent manner. Use and underline as many vocabulary words from this chapter as possible.

1743	Born in Paris, France
1754–1761	Attended the College Mazarin, studying chemistry, botany, astronomy, and mathematics
1764	Authored his first chemical publication
1767	Worked on a geological survey of Alsace-Lorraine in France
1768	Selected as a member of the French Academy of Sciences
1771	Married a 13-year-old girl who translated from English into French for him and illustrated his books
1775	Served on the Royal Gunpowder Administration
1779	Named oxygen as the combustible component of air
1787	Described a chemical system of names, which became the foundation of the modern system
1789	Published the first modern chemical textbook, which contributed a unified view of new theories of chemistry and featured
	• a clear statement of the law of conservation of mass
	• clarification of the concept of an element as a simple substance
	• a theory of the formation of chemical compounds from elements
1794	Implicated as a traitor by French revolutionaries and beheaded

http://www.nationmaster.com/encyclopedia/Antoine-Lavoisier

7B Paragraph Writing

Write a response to **one** of the following topics. Include at least **six to eight vocabulary words** in your paragraph.

1. Carbon monoxide has no taste, odor, or color. Yet it is a poisonous gas that kills many people each year, especially in the winter when windows are closed and heating systems and other appliances that use fossil fuels are being used every day. Write a paragraph highlighting precautions people should take to prevent carbon monoxide poisoning in the home. The following are some of the precautions that can be taken; be sure to include several ideas of your own as well.

   • Have chimneys checked.

   • Have a licensed professional check all fuel-burning appliances.

   • Install appliances according to the manufacturers' instructions.

   • Never warm up a car in the garage.

   • Never use a gas oven to heat a home.

   • Never use a charcoal grill indoors.

   • Install a carbon monoxide detector.

2. Write a short description of a chemistry fact that is *good, bad,* or *odd.* Describe the item, including its chemical composition, any chemical reactions associated with it, and its use in everyday life. Be sure to include any safety recommendations if the reaction is dangerous or an anecdote if it is good or odd.

8. SPEAKING

8A Partner Activity: Explaining a Chemistry Concept

It is common practice to designate the relative acidity or basicity of a solution by citing its pH (power of hydrogen) level. A pH of 7 indicates a neutral solution. Values from 6 down to 1 indicate increasing acidity, with each drop of one in value meaning a tenfold increase in acidity. Similarly, pH values from 8 up to 15 indicate increasing basicity, with each increase of one in value meaning a tenfold increase in basicity. The following diagram illustrates this concept and shows the pH values of some common solutions.

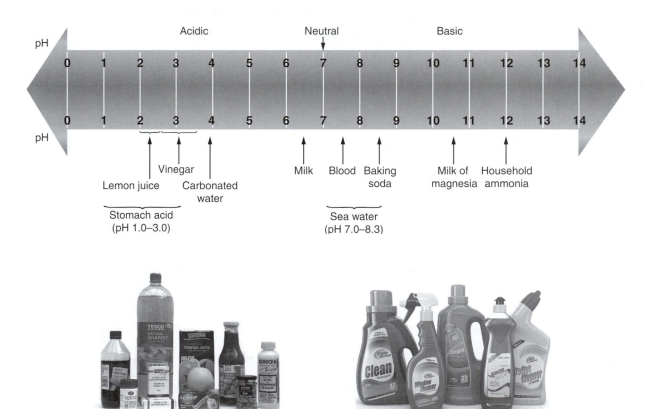

Reprinted with permission from James T. Shipman, Jerry D. Wilson, and Aaron W. Todd, *An Introduction to Physical Science*, 10th ed. (Boston: Houghton Mifflin, 2003), 332.

Orally describe the diagram to a partner, sequencing the information in a logical way.

- Explain the meaning of pH.

- Describe the range of the chart and what the values indicate.

- Highlight the products indicated on the diagram, explaining what each one is used for, if necessary.

- Add two more products to the chart and estimate their level of acidity (for example, orange juice, tomatoes, soap, dishwashing liquid).

- Deduce what might happen if a person had a blood pH lower than 7 or higher than 8. How can pH level be utilized by medical practitioners?

8B Conducting an Interview

Choose one of the following interview situations. Prepare for your interview by listing **six to eight** specific questions to ask. Conduct the interview, take notes on the responses, and report the results of the interview to a partner or the class. Note: See *Chapter 4* for a list of polite expressions useful in conducting interviews.

	Questions	Answers
1.		
2.		
3.		
4.		
5.		
6.		
7.		
8.		

1. You are taking a required course in chemistry this semester, and you are finding the course difficult. You face the prospect of failing the course because you just can't remember the formulas and abbreviations for the names of chemicals. Interview a student majoring in chemistry or a chemistry professor to get advice on the best ways to memorize the material and pass the course. Ask if there are any possibilities for getting chemistry tutoring.

2. Visit your campus careers center and consult a staff member about careers available for chemistry majors. Ask about the type of jobs available for people with undergraduate and graduate degrees in chemistry, the job security and prospects for professional advancement, the range of salaries in these jobs, and the personal characteristics suited to these job situations. Find out if the careers center will provide assistance for résumé writing, interviewing skills, and job placement.

| Address: | http://elt.heinle.com/essentialvocab | ▸ go |

For more activities related to this chapter, go to the *Essential Academic Vocabulary* website.

INFORMATION SCIENCE AND TECHNOLOGY

WORD LIST

Noun	Verb	Adjective	Adverb
advocate	accompany	arbitrary	conversely
chart	adjust	civilian	
consent	amend	concurrent	
criteria (pl.)	appreciate	explicit	
discrimination	assure	rigid	
file	cease	straightforward	
gender	commence	technical	
index	compile		
insight	contradict		
integrity	convince		
mode	deny		
reluctance	draft		
restoration	mediate		
route	negate		
sphere	prohibit		
theme	reinforce		
topic	sum		

PREVIEW QUESTIONS

1. What is meant by privacy in the context of the digital age? What is the controversy surrounding digital privacy?

2. When you make a purchase online, do you worry about credit card security? Do you think that information about your purchase is kept private or that it may be distributed to other businesses?

3. Do you get a lot of unsolicited e-mail that advertises products similar to others that you have purchased online in the past? How do advertisers obtain your e-mail address? Do you ever buy items from these advertisements?

4. How do you feel about your name and consumer history being given or sold to other businesses? Do you find this practice ethical? How can you prevent your data from being obtained by others?

5. Do you think that the government also has access to personal information about you obtained from your Internet purchases and surfing habits? Could this information be used against you?

6. How do you expect the issue of digital privacy to be resolved in the future?

READING

PRIVACY IN THE DIGITAL AGE

1   Critics' concerns about the World Wide Web are not limited to what companies deliver to people's computers via their websites and e-mail. The concerns also extend to what the companies often try to take from people as they use their computers. At issue is the information that web firms want about the individuals and organizations with whom they interact.

5   Companies are not the only targets of these worries. Activists fear that governments—federal or state—might enact laws that give them **arbitrary** powers to tap into people's computers or Internet activities. Officials from police agencies such as the Federal Bureau of Investigation (FBI) have already tried to prevent Internet software from helping potential criminals make their e-mail totally untraceable by law-enforcement authorities. After the 2001 attacks on the World

10   Trade Center and Pentagon, members of Congress **drafted** laws aimed at allowing the FBI and other agencies to trace digital **routes** more easily than in earlier years. However, Congress allowed the laws to expire two years later so that they could reevaluate and **amend** the laws if necessary.

    In general, concerned individuals and organizations argue that we are moving into a new information age. It is a period, they say, in which governments will be able to **compile** far more

15   information about citizens than the citizens want them to know. It is also a time when companies will be able to find out far more about their customers than those customers **appreciate**. In the new digital age, the critics **assure** us, **reinforcing** privacy must be a priority.

    This **theme** has become a media issue only rather recently. In earlier times, privacy was often defined as "the right to be let alone," to quote Samuel Warren and Louis Brandeis in a famous

20   1890 *Harvard Law Review* article. In the twenty-first century, privacy has become a **topic** that people debate when they are worried about governments, employers, or credit companies making **technical** invasions into their personal lives.

    In the past 15 years or so, concern about **civilian** privacy has erupted noisily into the media **sphere**. Most of the noise has related to corporate rather than government activities because of a

25   belief that laws are less **rigid** with regard to business interference. The first signs of concern

commenced in the 1970s, when companies began to use computers to combine enormous amounts of information from public and private records about virtually everyone in the country and sell this information to marketers. Many marketers use these firms' universal databases (so-called because they hold information on almost everyone) to find people whose characteristics
30 make them potential customers.

Donnelley's Conquest/Direct database, for example, offers marketers the **files** of 90 percent of all U.S. households by demographic **criteria** (for example, age, **gender**, race, job, number of children, marital status), lifestyle activities (for example, financial investments, hobbies, vacations taken, vehicles owned), sales expenses, and creditworthiness. Its software allows clients to
35 generate customized color **charts** of their market areas to see how the people who live there fit into these categories.

Many other companies offer other types of universal database services to help marketers identify prospects. The Carol Wright database, for example, covers 30 million households. For each household, the **index** includes information about dress size, pets owned, veteran status, type
40 of aspirin preferred, and other such information.

In addition to this bulk of knowledge, marketers themselves have been **adjusting** to the constantly decreasing costs of computer power by creating their databases from information they learn themselves about their customers, by asking them directly and by keeping records of their purchases. These storehouses of information are called transactional databases. A marketer that
45 wants more **explicit** information about the customers in its transactional database can turn to a company such as Database America. This company will match the names and addresses of the marketer's customers against its data on more than 84 million households. The resulting merged file could supply the marketer with a wealth of **concurrent** information about each customer's purchasing behavior, estimated income, credit extended by mail-order firms, investments, credit
50 cards, and more.

According to **advocates** of Internet tracking, it is an excellent way to gain **insight** about what users want and how best to serve them. Moreover, the managers of websites see the ability to target content and ads to individuals based on the computer's knowledge of these individuals' interests and past behavior as crucial to their competitive advantage over magazines and cable
55 television when it comes to attracting advertisers. **Conversely**, however, privacy advocates point out that tracking personal behavior, on or off the web, is often done without the knowledge or **consent** of the consumer.

Media executives rarely argue publicly that people should be **denied** the right to request firms to **cease** collecting information about them. Under government pressures, many often
60 admit that members of the public should have the right to know that material about them is being collected. Media executives emphasize, however, that in today's competitive media world, being able to show advertisers that a medium can deliver specific, desirable types of people is crucial for their survival. Supporters of data collection also claim that the invasion of privacy has its positive side. They argue that the more marketers know about people, the more they will be
65 able to **convince** individuals that the materials they send are relevant to their lives. The result, they say, is that people will be unlikely to complain that they receive junk mail.

Nowadays, most web marketers say that they understand people's **reluctance** to have certain information made public. They also insist, however, that many individuals are willing to give up information about themselves if in return they get something that they consider valuable. Many
70 privacy advocates agree that people should have the right to decide whether they want to provide

information as part of a transaction. They disagree with the web marketers on the **mode** of information retrieval. Privacy advocates want members of the public to have to *opt-in* when it comes to giving out information. That is, marketers should be **prohibited** from collecting information about a person unless that person explicitly consents (perhaps by checking a box online). Marketers contend that getting opt-in permission is too difficult because people are either too lazy to give it or are concerned about their privacy. The marketers prefer an *opt-out* approach. That means that they will be permitted to collect personal information from consumers as long as they inform people and give them the opportunity to check a "no" box or **negate** permission in some other way.

Privacy advocates are voicing increasing public concern about the **restoration** of privacy in the digital sphere. However, industry representatives **contradict** these concerns by insisting that interactive sites and marketers can regulate themselves. **Accompanying** these arguments is the international nature of the issue. The European Union (EU) uses an opt-in approach, for example, and U.S. companies have to promise to accept the more rigid EU rules when they deal with European customers. This **discrimination** angers U.S. advocates, who perceive the European approach as the one that shows the greatest **integrity**. To **sum** up, it is clear that the continuing fight over privacy in the digital age will not be a **straightforward** issue to **mediate** and resolve.

Adapted from Joseph Turow, *Media Today: An Introduction to Mass Communication*, 2nd ed. (Boston: Houghton Mifflin, 2003), 529–32.

1. VOCABULARY IN CONTEXT

Find the boldface words in the reading that correspond to the following meanings.

Paragraph 2	a. _____	change
	b. _____	without good reason
Paragraph 3	c. _____	declare positively
	d. _____	collect
Paragraph 5	e. _____	domain
	f. _____	strict
Paragraph 6	g. _____	sex
	h. _____	diagram
Paragraph 8	i. _____	at the same time
	j. _____	detailed

Paragraph 9	k. _____	agreement
	l. _____	supporters
Paragraph 10	m. _____	stop
	n. _____	persuade
Paragraph 11	o. _____	method
	p. _____	forbidden
	q. _____	unwillingness
Paragraph 12	r. _____	honesty
	s. _____	recovery
	t. _____	intervene

2. READING COMPREHENSION

2A Getting the Facts

1. Check the two statements that are true according to paragraph 1.

   a. _____ Critics are worried about people accessing business websites without permission.

   b. _____ Computer users are worried that data are unknowingly compiled about them.

   c. _____ People are concerned about unsolicited e-mail.

   d. _____ Web companies want to know which businesses people contact online.

2. According to the information in the second paragraph, what have the following groups done that privacy activists fear may lead to arbitrary invasions of privacy?

   a. Federal Bureau of Investigation _____

   _____

   b. members of Congress _____

   _____

3. Put a check mark (✓) next to each item of information specifically mentioned in paragraphs 6 and 7 that various marketers may know about individuals.

a. _____ clothing size	l. _____ marital status
b. _____ favorite colors	m. _____ level of education
c. _____ type of car owned	n. _____ preferred medicines
d. _____ number of children	o. _____ type of family pet
e. _____ job	p. _____ interests
f. _____ employment history	q. _____ military service
g. _____ shoe size	r. _____ year of birth
h. _____ sex	s. _____ vacation preferences
i. _____ salary	t. _____ financial investments
j. _____ savings account balance	u. _____ credit card history
k. _____ Christmas gifts	v. _____ amount of mortgage

4. In paragraph 8, transactional databases are described. Write a short definition of a transactional database.

   _____

   _____

   _____

5. Paragraphs 9, 10, and 11 deal with the arguments for and against Internet tracking. Complete the chart to show three components of the argument on both sides.

Advocates of Internet Tracking	Advocates of Privacy
1.	1.
2.	2.
3.	3.

6. Label the following statements as either an *opt-in* or an *opt-out* approach, as defined in paragraph 11.

   a. _____ The consumer is notified that information is being collected and has the opportunity to deny permission.

   b. _____ The consumer must check a box giving explicit permission to collect information.

7. According to the information in paragraph 12, which system do U.S. companies use when they do business?

   a. with Europeans _____ opt-in _____ opt-out

   b. with Americans _____ opt-in _____ opt-out

2B Making Inferences

1. In 1890, privacy was defined as "the right to be left alone." With the technical intrusions of today, how has this definition changed? What is a current definition of privacy?

_____

_____

2. The author of the reading states both sides of the argument on privacy. However, his choice of words and style may imply that he has a particular bias. What do you think is the author's opinion about digital privacy?

_____

_____

_____

You should continue to increase your vocabulary size and enrich the words you already know.

3. DICTIONARY SKILLS

Complete each sentence with the appropriate word(s) based on the dictionary entries.

civ•ic (sĭv′ĭk) *adj.* **1.** Relating to or belonging to a city: *Our town's Fourth of July parade is a major civic event.* **2.** Relating to citizenship: *It is a civic duty to vote in elections.*

civ•ics (sĭv′ĭks) *n.* [U] *(used with a singular verb).* The study of the purpose and function of local and national government and of the rights and duties of citizens.

civ•il (sĭv′əl) *adj.* **1.** Relating to a citizen or citizens: *voting and other civil responsibilities.* **2.** Relating to the general public rather than to military or religious matters: *a couple married in a civil ceremony at city hall.* **3.** Polite; courteous: *a civil reply.* See Synonyms at **polite.** —**civ′il•ly** *adv.*

civil engineer *n.* An engineer trained in the design and construction of bridges, roads, and dams. —**civil engineering** *n.* [U]

ci•vil•ian (sĭ vĭl′yən) *n.* A person not serving in the military. —*adj.* Relating to civilians: *civilian clothes; a civilian career.*

ci•vil•i•ty (sĭ vĭl′ĭ tē) *n., pl.* **ci•vil•i•ties. 1.** [U] Courteous behavior; politeness: *civility in daily life.* **2.** [C] An act or expression of politeness: *Saying "good morning" is a pleasant civility.*

civ•i•li•za•tion (sĭv′ə lĭ zā′shən) *n.* **1.** [U] A condition of human society in which there is a high level of development in the arts and sciences and political and social organizations: *Warfare is not consistent with the idea of civilization.* **2.** [C] The kind of culture and society developed by a particular people or nation in some period of history: *ancient civilizations.* **3.** [U] *Informal.* Modern society with its conveniences: *We were glad to return to civilization after two weeks of camping.*

civ•i•lize (sĭv′ə līz′) *tr.v.* **civ•i•lized, civ•i•liz•ing, civ•i•liz•es.** To bring (sbdy.) to a higher level of development in the arts, sciences, culture, and political organization.

civ•i•lized (sĭv′ə līzd′) *adj.* **1.** Having or marked by a highly developed society and culture: *civilized life.* **2.** Polite or cultured: *a civilized person.*

civil rights *pl.n.* The rights belonging to an individual as a citizen, especially freedom from discrimination.

civil servant *n.* A person employed in the civil service.

civil service *n.* **1.** [C] All branches of government service that are not legislative, judicial, or military. **2.** [U] Those persons employed by the civil branches of the government: *Most people in the civil service in the United States government are hired after competitive examinations.*

civil war *n.* **1.** [C] A war between opposing groups of the same country. **2. Civil War.** [U] The war in the United States between the North and the South from 1861 to 1865.

civic	civil	civil rights	civil wars	civilizations
civics	civil engineering	civil servants	civilians	civilized

1. _____ have to take difficult tests before being hired by the government.

2. Martin Luther King Jr. is well known as an advocate of _____, which refers to fair treatment under the law, regardless of race, gender, or religion.

3. Many cities try to increase _____ pride by holding festivals and planting flowers in the summer.

4. My sister has always been interested in the construction of bridges, so she is studying _____.

5. In times of war, the lives of _____ may be endangered even though they are not involved in the fighting.

6. Although Ben was angry about the invasion of his privacy by a web company, he tried to act in a _____ manner to resolve the problem.

7. High-school students generally take a course in _____ to learn more about the system of government and their responsibilities as citizens.

8. Historians and archaeologists still have much to learn about ancient _____ throughout the world.

9. My aunt is a very _____ person who loves to visit museums, attend plays, read the classics, and visit places of historical importance.

10. Several countries in Africa have been involved in _____ for many years, which have led to countless deaths, starvation, and political uncertainty.

4. WORD FORMS

4A Chart Completion

Complete the chart with the different forms of each word. Note that some words do not have all forms.

Noun	Verb	Adjective	Adverb
rigidity, rigidness	X	rigid	rigidly
	contradict		X
advocate		X	X
	X	explicit	
reluctance	X		
		concurrent	
			conversely
	negate		
	appreciate		
	assure		

4B Word Forms in Sentences

Reread paragraph 12 in "Privacy in the Digital Age." Complete a summary of the paragraph with the following words. Make sure that each word fits grammatically and meaningfully.

advocates	contradictory	explicit	priority	restoring
appreciate	discriminatory	mediation	prohibited	topic

(1) _____ of privacy are increasingly (2) _____ about their concern for (3) _____ privacy in the digital domain. However, (4) _____ statements from industry representatives claim that interactive sites and marketers can regulate themselves. The international nature of the issue accompanies this argument. The European Union uses an opt-in approach, so U.S. companies are (5) _____ from using the opt-out approach when they deal with European customers. U.S. advocates do not (6) _____ this (7) _____ approach because the European approach is considered to have more integrity. In summary, it is quite clear that the (8) _____ of privacy in the digital age should be a (9) _____ for (10) _____ and resolution by the government.

5. COLLOCATIONS

Give **two examples** of each of the following common collocations.

1. gender discrimination _____ _____
2. arbitrary rules _____ _____
3. civilian governments _____ _____
4. advertising prohibitions _____ _____
5. essay topics _____ _____
6. technical problems _____ _____
7. literary themes _____ _____
8. building restorations _____ _____
9. ancient civilizations _____ _____
10. transportation modes _____ _____
11. confidential files _____ _____
12. parental consent _____ _____
13. words of appreciation _____ _____

6. Word Parts

-voc- (speak, call)

6A Each of the following words includes the word part *-voc-*, which means "speak" or "call." Write each word in the box next to its meaning.

Nouns:	voice, advocacy, vocation, vocalist, convocation
Verbs:	invoke, revoke, vocalize, provoke
Adjectives:	vocal, irrevocable, vociferous

1. _____ expressing strong opinions publicly

2. _____ expressing strong opinions loudly (formal)

3. _____ the feeling that you are meant to help others in a particular job

4. _____ a large formal meeting

5. _____ unable to be stopped or amended

6. _____ someone who sings in a band

7. _____ the ability to produce oral sounds

8. _____ express an opinion orally

9. _____ public support for a cause

10. _____ make someone angry

11. _____ cause an idea or image to appear in someone's mind

12. _____ officially cancel

6B Write a sentence for each of the following terms with *-voc-* to clearly illustrate the meaning of the phrase.

1. a vocal critic _____

_____

2. vocal chords _____

_____

3. vocational training _____

_____

4. the passive voice _____

_____

5. voice mail _____

_____

6. provocative clothes _____

_____

7. provocative behavior _____

_____

8. irrevocable damage _____

_____

7. WRITING

7A Writing a Lab Guide

While working in a computer lab on campus, your supervisor has asked you to write guidelines to help students protect their privacy online. You have been given several points as the basis of your guide, but you need to include additional guidelines and specific details. Write a short guide with an interesting title for protecting online privacy.

- Do not respond to spam e-mail.

- Avoid revealing any personal information.

- Be knowledgeable about web security.

- Do not give personal information to people you meet online.

- Read privacy policies on websites you use.

7B Paragraph Writing

Write a response to **one** of the following topics. Include at least **six to eight vocabulary words** in your paragraph.

1. Write a paragraph describing any experiences you have had with violations of online privacy. How do you feel about releasing credit card information online? Are you aware that private information about you may be on databases that are sold to companies? What kind of information about you do you think might be on their databases? Do you know how to make your private information more secure?

2. Spam mail is taking up increasing amounts of space in our mailboxes and is often objectionable in content. How do you feel about this unsolicited mail, and how do you deal with it—do you read it or trash it? What can parents do to stop their children from receiving and opening sexually explicit e-mail or advertisements for inappropriate products? How do you anticipate that the privacy issue regarding spam e-mail will be resolved in the future?

8. SPEAKING

8A Group Project: Online Privacy Survey

In small groups, prepare the survey together by writing **ten** statements relevant to Internet privacy issues. The chart will help you get started. Then each group member should survey six to eight people on how they feel about these issues. Record their responses as Agree, Don't Know, or Disagree.

	Survey Statements	Agree	Don't Know	Disagree
1.	I don't know much about Internet privacy.			
2.	I usually give out personal information on the Internet when I'm asked for it.			
3.				
4.				
5.				
6.				
7.				
8.				
9.				
10.				

Compile the results of your survey. In your group, compare and contrast the information each group member has gathered. Summarize your combined results and give a short report to the class. Emphasize any clear patterns of responses and indicate any areas of concern for Internet users.

8B Role-Plays

Using new vocabulary words from this chapter, act out the following role-plays.

1. You have just realized that online companies probably know a lot about you from your recent online purchases. You are angry because you did not consent to this information being taken from you. You complain about this situation to a friend who is majoring in information science and technology. Tell your friend what kinds of information about you might be in a database and ask for advice about protecting your online privacy in the future.

2. You have been receiving increasing amounts of advertising and sexually explicit spam e-mail lately. You are worried that your 10-year-old daughter is going to read this information, but you don't want to prohibit her from using the Internet because she needs to use the Internet for school projects. Call your Internet provider and ask for advice on how to block the spam and how to make sure that you receive e-mail only from people you know.

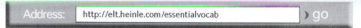

Address: http://elt.heinle.com/essentialvocab   › go

For more activities related to this chapter, go to the *Essential Academic Vocabulary* website.

CHAPTER 20

CUMULATIVE REVIEW

PREVIEW SENTENCES

What do you know about how we process speech? Test your knowledge by deciding whether the following statements are true (**T**) or false (**F**).

1. _____ The process of understanding speech sounds is complex.

2. _____ Speech recognition software can easily comprehend human speech.

3. _____ The sounds of a specific letter vary depending on the sounds that follow them.

4. _____ Everyone speaks in the same way.

5. _____ In real speech, words tend to be joined together.

6. _____ Voice-recognition software is always accurate.

7. _____ Knowing the context of a message helps people understand the meaning.

8. _____ Nonverbal language rarely provides important information in a message.

9. _____ Body language can be stronger than verbal language.

10. _____ It is easier to understand someone talking on the telephone than face-to-face.

1. VOCABULARY IN CONTEXT

Write the appropriate word from each group of words in the numbered blanks in the reading.

1. reconstruct, reject, release
2. emphasizes, enables, enhances
3. policy, process, promotion
4. highlights, involves, reinforces
5. complex, crucial, explicit
6. decades, fluctuations, layers
7. accuracy, controversy, discrimination
8. factor, mode, priority
9. external, physical, practical
10. furthermore, nevertheless, thereby

11. adjust, amend, differentiate
12. albeit, despite, thereby
13. conclusions, errors, transformations
14. challenges, guidelines, scenarios
15. analyzing, enforcing, sustaining
16. exposures, features, incentives
17. allocate, identify, substitute
18. dynamic, individual, virtual
19. confer, detect, undergo
20. somewhat, via, whereby

UNDERSTANDING SPEECH

When someone speaks to you in your own language, your sensory, perceptual, and other cognitive systems (1) _____ the sounds of speech in a way that (2) _____ you to detect, recognize, and understand what the person is saying. The (3) _____ may seem effortless, but it (4) _____ amazingly (5) _____ acts of information processing. Scientists trying to develop speech-recognition software systems have discovered how complex the process is. After (6) _____ of effort, the (7) _____ and efficiency of these systems are still not much better than those of the average five-year-old child. What makes understanding speech so complicated?

One (8) _____ is that the (9) _____ features of a particular speech sound are not always the same. The sounds of specific letters differ depending on the sounds that follow them. A second factor complicating our comprehension of speech is that each of us creates slightly different speech sounds, even when saying the same words. (10) _____, as people speak, their words are not usually separated by silence, so it is often difficult to (11) _____ the beginning and endings of words.

(12) _____ these challenges, humans can instantly recognize and understand the words and sentences produced by almost anyone speaking a familiar language. In contrast, even the best voice-recognition software must learn to recognize words spoken by a new voice and even then may make many (13) _____.

Scientists have yet to discover all the details about how people overcome the (14) _____ of understanding speech, but some general answers are emerging. Just as we recognize objects by (15) _____ their visual (16) _____, it appears that humans (17) _____ and recognize the specific—and changing—characteristics of the sounds created when someone speaks. Context and expectation, such as knowing the general topic of conversation, helps us to recognize (18) _____ words that might otherwise be hard to understand.

Finally, we are often guided to an understanding of speech by nonverbal cues. The frown, the enthusiastic nod, or the bored yawn that accompanies speech—each carries information that helps us understand what the person is saying. So if someone says, "Wow, are you smart!" but really means "I think you're a jerk," we will (19) _____ the true meaning based on the context, facial expression, and tone of voice. No wonder it is usually easier to understand someone in a face-to-face conversation than on the telephone or (20) _____ e-mail.

_____

Adapted from Douglas A. Bernstein, Louis A. Penner, Alison Clarke-Stewart, and Edward J. Roy, *Psychology*, 6th ed. (Boston: Houghton Mifflin, 2003), 294–95.

2. SYNONYMS

Match each word in column A with its meaning in column B.

	Column A		Column B
1. _____	commence	a.	army, navy, air force
2. _____	bulk	b.	stiff, strict
3. _____	concurrent	c.	money
4. _____	manual	d.	begin
5. _____	military	e.	end
6. _____	rigid	f.	safety
7. _____	temporary	g.	choose
8. _____	currency	h.	a large quantity
9. _____	schedule	i.	results
10. _____	exploitation	j.	scholarly magazine
11. _____	termination	k.	plan of activities
12. _____	consequences	l.	at the same time
13. _____	select	m.	unfair treatment
14. _____	security	n.	short-term
15. _____	journal	o.	by hand

3. ODD WORD OUT

Cross out the word in each group that does NOT have a similar meaning to the other three words.

1. alter, modify, justify, adjust
2. partnership, profit, income, revenue
3. center, core, comment, middle
4. exterior, outside, external, explicit
5. prime, initial, parallel, first
6. goal, validity, target, objective
7. demonstration, occupation, job, task
8. series, sequence, cycle, shift
9. subsequent, following, concurrent, after
10. debate, document, discussion, conversation

4. WORD FORMS IN SENTENCES

4A   Use the correct italicized word form to meaningfully and grammatically complete the following sentences.

1. Teachers generally try to respond to the needs of their students, who learn _____ as well as inductively.
   deduction, deduce, deductive, deductively

2. Our new business will show only a _____ profit this year.
   margin, marginalize, marginal, marginally

3. It is the goal of the international conference to _____ relations between dissenting countries.
   norm, normalize, normal, normalization

4. _____ of the laws is not a valid excuse for committing crimes.
   ignorance, ignore, ignorant, ignorantly

5. Research involves the _____ analysis of a hypothesis.
   rationalization, rationalize, rational, rationally

6. At the _____ of her speech, Dr. Wang thanked the university president for inviting her to speak to the graduating students.
   conclusion, conclude, conclusive, conclusively

7. The professor spoke _____ about the forthcoming test and then continued with the planned lecture.
   brevity, brief, brief, briefly

8. The answers to the test questions must be written _____ and comprehensively.
   coherency, cohere, coherent, coherently

9. My brother has had a _____ cold for two weeks, but he is finally starting to recover from it.
   persistence, persist, persistent, persistently

10. Increasing _____ in industry has caused many manufacturing jobs to be lost.
    automation, automate, automatic, automatically

4B Give the correct noun form for each of the following verbs.

1. imply _____

2. memorize _____

3. subsidize _____

4. intensify _____

5. authorize _____

6. illustrate _____

7. promote _____

8. register _____

9. validate _____

10. hypothesize _____

11. organize _____

12. integrate _____

13. consume _____

14. terminate _____

15. emphasize _____

16. locate _____

17. justify _____

18. publish _____

19. opt _____

20. generate _____

5. COLLOCATIONS

Combine a word from column A with a word from column B to form a common collocation. Then match each two-word collocation with its definition.

Column A		Column B	
instruction	ancient	vocabulary	uniform
traffic	parental	scenario	mail
passive	gender	civilization	violation
school	legal	manual	consent
worst-case	registered	document	discrimination

1. _____ women being paid less than men for doing the same job

2. _____ secure delivery system for important letters and packages

3. _____ permission from a child's mother or father

4. _____ a book of directions for operating equipment

5. _____ a very old culture

6. _____ a birth certificate and a marriage certificate are typical examples

7. _____ a police citation for speeding

8. _____ knowledge of words for reading and listening

9. _____ required clothes worn by some children in educational institutions

10. _____ a possible serious problem that can be predicted

6. WORD PARTS

6A Complete the chart with the meaning of each word part and three examples of words that contain the word part.

	Word Part	Meaning	Three Examples
1.	-vis-, -vid-	see	vision, visualize, evidence
2.	-port-		
3.	mini-		
4.	multi-		
5.	-ology		
6.	psych-		
7.	trans-		
8.	-phon-		
9.	-aqua-		
10.	over-		
11.	-hydr-		
12.	-voc-		

6B Complete the chart with three additional examples of each adjective ending.

Adjective Suffixes	Three Examples
-al	loyal,
-ative, -ive	attentive,
-ent, -ant	dependent,
-ic	poetic,
-ish	boyish,
-ous, -ious	conscious,
-able	capable,

6C Complete the chart with three additional examples of each suffix denoting what a person does for employment or relaxation.

Job Noun Suffixes	Three Examples
-ian	musician,
-er	lawyer,
-or	director,
-ist	pianist,

6D Now use one word from each of the three charts to create **ten** original and meaningful sentences.

1. _The boyish lawyer found the evidence to convict the criminal._

2.

3.

4.

5.

6.

7.

8.

9.

10.

11.

7. VOCABULARY IN CONTEXT

Write the appropriate word beginning with the letters provided next to the numbered blanks in the text. Your completed answers should correspond to the synonyms in the following box.

Synonyms

1. questionnaire	7. add	13. remove	19. national
2. grown-ups	8. separate	14. control	20. demand
3. procedures	9. purchasers'	15. complicated	21. explicit
4. proof	10. most important parts	16. suggest	22. direct
5. largest number	11. answers	17. laws	23. meeting
6. methods	12. scope	18. entry	24. information

THE ONLINE PRIVACY CRISIS

A new national (1) survey_____ reveals that American (2) adults_____ who go online at home misunderstand the purpose of privacy (3) policies_____. The study is also the first to provide (4) evid_____ that the overwhelming (5) maj_____ of U.S. adults who use the Internet at home have no clue about the flow of data—the invisible (6) tech_____ whereby online organizations extract, manipulate, (7) appe_____, profile, and share information about users. Even if they have an idea that websites track them and collect (8) indi_____ bits of their data, users simply do not comprehend how those bits can be used. In fact, when presented with a common way that sites currently handle (9) cons_____ information, people say they find it unacceptable.

   The (10) high_____ of the survey (11) resp_____ raise questions about the usefulness of trying to educate American consumers in the growing (12) ran_____ of tools needed to protect their online information at a time when technologies to (13) extr_____ and (14) mani_____ that information are themselves growing and becoming increasingly (15) comp_____. The findings (16) indi_____ that consumers want (17) legi_____ that will help them easily gain (18) acc_____ to and control over all information collected about them online. The results also suggest that the (19) fed_____ government needs to (20) requ_____ online organizations to provide (21) unamb_____ disclosures about their information-collection policies as well as to provide (22) strai_____ explanations at the start of every online (23) enc_____ about how the (24) dat_____ will be used.

Adapted from *Americans Online Privacy: The System Is Broken*. A Report from the Annenberg Public Policy Center of the University of Pennsylvania, http://www.appcpenn.org/04_info_society/2003_online_privacy_version_09.pdf.

Address: | http://elt.heinle.com/essentialvocab | ▸ go

For more activities related to this chapter, go to the *Essential Academic Vocabulary* website.

APPENDIX I

GETTING THE MOST FROM YOUR DICTIONARY

Elements of the Dictionary

B The symbol for the element **boron.** ——————— symbol entry

Ba The symbol for the element **barium.**

B.A. *abbr.* An abbreviation of Bachelor of Arts. ——————— abbreviation entry

entry word ——— **back•ward** (băk′wərd) *adj.* **1.** In the direction of the rear: *a backward glance; a backward tumble.* **2.** Less advanced than others, as in economic or social progress: *backward technology. -adv.* or **back•wards**

definition ——— (băk′wərdz). **1.** To or toward the back or rear: *He kept glancing backward to see who was coming.* **2.** With the back or rear first: *With its hind legs a toad can dig its way into the ground backward.* **3.** In reverse order or direction: *count backward from 100.* **4.** Toward a worse condition: *As prices rise, poor people slip backward.* ◆

idiom ——— **bend over backward.** To make an effort greater than is required: *They bent over backward to be fair.* **know backward and forward** or **backwards and forwards.** To know sthg. very well or perfectly: *We know the play backward and forward.*

part-of-speech label ——— **bad** (băd) *adj.* **worse** (wûrs), **worst** (wûrst). **1.** Being below an acceptable standard; poor: *a bad book; a bad painter.* **2.** Evil or wicked: *a bad man.* **3.** Disobedient; naughty: *bad behavior.* **4.** Unfavorable: *bad luck; bad weather.* **5.** Disagreeable or unpleasant: *a bad odor; bad news.* **6.** Incorrect; improper: *a bad choice of words.* **7.** Not working properly; defective: *a bad telephone connection. -n.* [U] Something bad: *You must learn to accept the bad with the good.* ◆ **not half bad** or **not so bad.** *Informal.* Reasonably good: *That meal was not half bad.* **too bad.** Regrettable; unfortunate: *It's too bad you can't come along.* **-bad′ness** *n.* [U] ——————— uncountable label

——— uncountable label (right, sense 7)

Usage Note ——— **USAGE: bad** You should avoid using **bad** as an adverb. Instead of *We need water bad,* use *We need water badly.* Instead of *My tooth hurt bad,* use *My tooth hurt badly.*

HOMONYMS: bad, bade (past of bid). ——————— homonyms

usage label ——— **bal•lis•tics** (bə lĭs′tĭks) *n.* [U] *(used with a singular verb).* The scientific study of the characteristics of projectiles, such as bullets or missiles, and the way they move in flight.

bal•loon (bə loon′) *n.* **1.** A large flexible bag filled with helium, hot air, or some other

pronunciation ——— gas that is lighter than the surrounding air and designed to rise and float in the atmosphere, often with a gondola or scientific instruments. **2.** A small brightly colored rubber or plastic bag that is inflated and used as a toy. **3.** A rounded or irregularly shaped outline containing the words that a character in a cartoon is represented to be saying. *-intr.v.* **1.** To swell out like a baloon: *The tire ballooned as it was inflated with air.* **2.** To ride in a gondola suspended from a balloon: *scenic ballooning over the town.* ——— art

symbol ——— **bar•i•um** (băr′ē əm *or* băr′ē əm) *n.* [U] *Symbol* **Ba** A soft, silvery-white, metallic element that occurs only in combination with other elements. Barium compounds are used in making pigments and safety matches. Atomic number 56. See table at **element.** ——————— table cross-reference

balloon
Hot-air balloons ——— caption

inflected forms ——— **be•gin** (bĭ gĭn′) *v.* **be•gan** (bĭ găn′), **be•gun** (bĭ gŭn′), **be•gin•ning, be•gins.** *-intr.* **1.** To take the first step in doing sthg.; start; commence: *We began with the kitchen and cleaned the whole house.* **2.** To come into being; originate: *Education begins at home.* **3.** To accomplish in the least way; come near: *The little bit of*

example ——— *paint won't begin to cover the ceiling. -tr.* **1.** To start doing (sthg.): *If we begin our work now, we'll have time to enjoy ourselves later.* **2.** To bring (sthg.) into being; originate: *The owner's grandfather began the newspaper many years ago.* **3.** To come first in (sthg.): *The letter A begins the alphabet.*

be•sides (bĭ sī[mc]dz′) *adv.* In addition; also: *We had dinner and a late-night snack besides. -prep.* In addition to: *Dentists do other things besides drilling cavities.* —See Note at **together.** ——————— Note cross-reference

Synonym Note ——— **SYNONYMS: besides, too, also, likewise, furthermore.** These adverbs mean in addition to sthg. else. **Besides** often introduces sthg. that reinforces what has gone before it: *We don't feel like cooking; besides, there is no food in the house.* **Too** is the most casual, used in everyday speech: *If you're going to the library today, I'd like to go too.* **Also** is more formal than **too:** *My brother is usually very friendly, but he is also capable of holding a grudge.* **Likewise** is even more formal: *Their parents were likewise attending the ceremony.* **Furthermore** often stresses the clause following it as more important than the clause before it: *I don't want you to go to that place; furthermore, I forbid it.*

prefix entry ——— **bio–** or **bi–** *pref.* A prefix that means: **1.** Life or living organism: *biography.* **2.** Biology or biological: *biophysics.*

WORD BUILDING: bio– The prefix **bio–** means "life." When used to form words in English, **bio–** generally refers to living organisms or to biology, the science of living organisms. Many of the words that begin with **bio–,** such as **bioethics** and **biotechnology,** have only come into being in the 20th century. Sometimes before an *o* **bio–** becomes **bi–: biopsy.** ——— Word Building Note

status label ——— **breath•er** (brē′thər) *n. Informal.* A short period of rest: *After this chore, let's take a breather.*

221

Study the preceding dictionary page. Choose the word or phrase that completes each of the following sentences.

1. A synonym for *besides* is _____.
   a. next to
   b. beside
   c. furthermore

2. *Bad* is a(n) _____.
   a. adverb
   b. adjective
   c. verb

3. The symbol for the element *barium* is _____.
   a. B
   b. Ba
   c. B.A.

4. The prefix *bio-* means _____.
   a. two
   b. again
   c. life

5. The word *breather* is used _____.
   a. in informal situations
   b. in formal situations
   c. rarely

6. The verb *begin* is _____.
   a. transitive
   b. intransitive
   c. both transitive and intransitive

7. The opposite of *backward* is _____.
   a. ballistics
   b. forward
   c. start

8. *Breather* rhymes with _____.
   a. leather
   b. father
   c. freezer

9. *Begin*, *commence*, and *start* are _____.
   a. antonyms
   b. synonyms
   c. homonyms

10. *Balloon* is a _____.
    a. verb
    b. noun
    c. verb and a noun

11. *Ballistics* takes a _____.
    a. singular verb
    b. plural verb
    c. passive verb

12. *Not half bad* means _____.
    a. excellent
    b. terrible
    c. fairly good

13. The word with the most syllables is _____.
    a. backward
    b. besides
    c. barium

14. *Bend over backward* is a(n) _____.
    a. idiom
    b. part of speech
    c. definition

15. The adjective *bad* has _____.
    a. 1 meaning
    b. 7 meanings
    c. 11 meanings

16. *Badness* has _____.
    a. three syllables
    b. no plural form
    c. two meanings

17. B.A. is a(n) _____.
    a. abbreviation
    b. symbol
    c. caption

18. The word *biotechnology* includes a _____.
    a. verb
    b. plural form
    c. prefix

APPENDIX II

SUGGESTIONS FOR LEARNING AND REVIEWING VOCABULARY

Each chapter in this textbook introduces thirty to forty words from the Academic Word List. Some of these words may be familiar to you, while others may be unfamiliar to you. The definitions of these words are not provided for you in the text. Therefore, you must learn to use an English-English dictionary (a monolingual English dictionary for ESL learners) effectively to extract a variety of useful information about the words; this information should be written down and reviewed from time to time to help you commit the words to long-term memory. Using **vocabulary cards** and **vocabulary notebooks** are two effective methods of clearly organizing vocabulary. Try both methods and choose the method that works best for you.

A complete entry on a vocabulary card or in a vocabulary notebook might contain the following information, all of which can be found in a dictionary:

- word meaning, explanation, or synonym with an optional translation
- multiple meanings of the same word
- illustration of the meaning to help visualize the word
- phonetic pronunciation
- any spelling irregularities (e.g., plural forms)
- other word forms (noun, verb, adjective, adverb)
- prefixes and suffixes included in the word
- prefixes and suffixes that can be added to form new words
- collocations (words that are commonly used together)
- formal or informal style
- positive or negative connotations
- topic associations
- an original sentence

VOCABULARY CARDS

You can make vocabulary cards from index cards, either white or colored. Vocabulary cards have many advantages because they are easy to carry around, can be placed in any order for review or practice, and can be posted in convenient locations for review. Study the following sample vocabulary card. (*Important note*: Not all words in a dictionary provide the same amount of information. Some entries will be shorter or longer than this one.)

Word	Illustration
AMBIGUITY	

Meaning	Original sentence
the condition of having more than one meaning.	*The ambiguity of this test question makes me unsure how to answer it.*

Part of Speech	Associations
ambiguity—noun	*meanings words*
Pronunciation	*ambiguity*
(ăm' bĭ gyōo ĭ tē) *n.,*	*remarks ideas*
Related word forms	**Collocations**
ambiguous—adj.	*the ambiguity of words*
unambiguous—adj. (antonym)	*ambiguous remarks*
ambiguities—pl.	*ambiguities in an essay*
ambi- = both	

Sample Vocabulary Card

VOCABULARY NOTEBOOK

Some people prefer to use a vocabulary notebook to record and review vocabulary. Choose a medium-sized notebook—a small one may be difficult to organize clearly, and a large one may be difficult to carry around easily. The same information that is recorded on vocabulary cards can be recorded in a vocabulary notebook. The following example is one way to organize your vocabulary information in a notebook.

ambiguity (n)	Meaning	the condition of having mo... than one meaning
(Illustration)	Sentence	The ambiguity of this test question makes me unsure how to answer it.
	Pronunciation	(am' bi gyoo i te) n.,
	Related word	ambiguous (adj.)
	Forms	unambiguous (adj.) (antonym
	Spelling	ambiguities (pl.)
	Word part	ambi- = both
	Associations	meanings, words, ideas, remarks.
	Collocations	the ambiguity of words ambiguous remarks ambiguities in an essay

Sample Vocabulary Notebook Page

REVIEWING VOCABULARY

It usually takes from five to fifteen reviews or uses of a single word to commit the word to memory. Therefore, you should regularly review both previous and new vocabulary. It is best to review new words immediately after writing them down. Then gradually increase the period of time between reviews until you feel that you have thoroughly learned the words. Here are some methods you can try:

- Look away from the card or notebook when reviewing—do not just read it.

- Say the words and meanings aloud.

- Practice with a partner.

- Think of different categories to place the words in.

- Use the words in new sentences related to your own experiences.

- Use the new words in other classes and assignments.

Appendix III

TECHNIQUES FOR PARAPHRASING

Paraphrasing is an important academic writing skill. Paraphrasing is used to express the same ideas or information as the original text but with different vocabulary and grammar structures. Paraphrasing is frequently used to include information from other sources in research papers, along with the correct attribution of the original source material.

A good paraphrase

- uses different grammar structures,

- uses synonyms and expressions with similar meanings,

- is approximately the same length as the original,

- includes the same ideas as the original, AND

- includes correct documentation of the source (author, title, journal/book, date, etc.) if the source is published material.

(Documentation is not included in the following because these examples do not have a specific source.)

EXAMPLE 1

Original:

- Although the artist encountered many difficulties in his life, he became extremely well known and successful.

Possible paraphrases:

- The painter was a popular success despite experiencing many problems during his lifetime.

- The artist had many problems during his lifetime; nonetheless, he experienced considerable recognition and success.

- Despite the fact that he had experienced many hardships, the artist had a successful and distinguished career.

- The painter achieved fame and success, his many problems notwithstanding.

EXAMPLE 2

Original:

- The persistent errors made by the accountant caused the business to fail.

Possible paraphrases:

- The accountant always made so many mistakes that eventually the company had to close down.
- The failure of the company was the consequence of the accountant's repeated miscalculations.
- As a result of the long-standing incompetence of the accountant, the firm went bankrupt.
- The bankruptcy of the company was due to the repeated mistakes of the accountant.

PRACTICE

A. Read each sentence and choose the paraphrase that most closely matches its meaning. Then state the reasons for your choice.

1. Test anxiety can cause nervousness, memory loss, and an inability to concentrate.
   a. Test anxiety may cause nervousness, loss of memory, and lack of concentration.
   b. Feelings of nervousness, forgetfulness, and a loss of ability to study are all signs of exam stress.
   c. Students who are nervous about exams experience more loss of memory.

   _____

   _____

2. Many college professors give their students cooperative-learning assignments that encourage them to work together as a team.
   a. Professors try to encourage team building by assigning group projects.
   b. According to professors, students who study together experience greater benefits.
   c. Team building projects assigned by university professors reinforce cooperative ways of learning among students.

   _____

   _____

B. Paraphrase the following sentences, using different vocabulary and grammar structures wherever possible.

1. Students who live off-campus often have positive experiences if they have realistic expectations of their roommates and landlord.

   _____

   _____

   _____

2. Many people immigrate to the United States to find better jobs, higher salaries, and more opportunities for their families.

_____

_____

_____

3. Currently, major corporations manufacture and market their products all over the world.

_____

_____

_____

4. Diamond engagement rings are advertised to consumers as symbols of wealth and love.

_____

_____

_____

5. Studies have shown that people in all cultures show similar facial expressions in response to specific emotions.

_____

_____

_____

Appendix IV

TECHNIQUES FOR SUMMARIZING

A summary is a shortened version of another person's words or ideas in a book, an article, or a lecture. Summarizing is an important academic writing skill for writing lecture notes, answering short essay questions, and writing the main points of a speech or text. Summarizing is also frequently used to include information, in a much shorter format, from other sources in research papers, along with the correct documentation *(see Appendix III)*.

A good summary

- includes only the main points, not the details;

- does not change the author's ideas;

- does not include your own opinion;

- is much shorter than the original text;

- is written or paraphrased in your own words; AND

- is written in the third person with occasional references to the source.

HOW TO SUMMARIZE

- Read the text several times to make sure you understand it.

- Find the topic sentence (usually the first sentence) and any other key points in each paragraph. If you own the publication, you can underline or highlight these key points.

- Write your own summary, paraphrasing the main points. Make sure you use your own words and vary the grammatical structures.

- Include a reference to the author and title of the article at the beginning of the summary, for example,

  According to John Stewart in his article, "The Hurried Life," people are so concerned with making money that they forget the value of quiet moments.

- Include one or more verbs that indicate a reference to a source, for example,

  The author argues (*suggests, states, concludes, questions, says, reports, tells, asks*) that . . .

1. Summarizing a Paragraph

Read the following paragraph from "Shifting Challenges in Education" in chapter 6. Then read the sample summary of the paragraph. Pay special attention to the author and title references in boldface type.

Original Paragraph

In that first decade of her professional career, however, demographic shifts took place in California. Los Angeles expanded and its suburbs multiplied, and her community became a popular location for recently arrived Mexican immigrants and other Spanish-speaking people coming to California from towns and cities in the southwestern United States. Correspondingly, the proportions of white and minority children in Mrs. Tanner's fifth grade class also began to change. Her white, middle-class students were joined by African American children whose parents had relocated from the southern United States and by children who spoke Spanish in their working-class homes and commuted regularly between the United States and Mexico. The parents of these children, like the grandparents of her earlier students, had come to the United States to find employment with sufficient financial compensation to ensure a higher standard of living for their families.

Adapted from Eugene Garcia, *Student Cultural Diversity: Understanding and Meeting the Challenge,* 3rd ed. (Boston: Houghton Mifflin, 2002), 4–5.

Sample Summary

According to Eugene Garcia in *Student Cultural Diversity: Understanding and Meeting the Challenge,* significant changes in the student population in Mrs. Tanner's school began to occur in the first ten years of her teaching career as greater numbers of African Americans and Mexicans arrived in Los Angeles to seek a better life.

2. Summarizing an Article

Read the article "Shifting Challenges in Education" in chapter 6. Next read the main ideas of each paragraph. Then read the sample summary of the article. Pay special attention to the author and title references in boldface type.

Main Ideas

Paragraph 1   Mrs. Tanner is a fifth-grade teacher in a typical elementary school in southern California.

Paragraph 2   When Mrs. Tanner began teaching in 1981, her students had a background similar to her own, and thus she emphasized active participation to promote academic achievement.

Paragraph 3   Significant changes in the student population in her school began to occur in the first ten years of her teaching career as greater numbers of African Americans and Mexicans arrived in Los Angeles to seek a better life.

Paragraph 4   New arrivals of immigrants from all over the world, escaping from economic and political instability in their own countries, continued to add to the ethnic diversity of her students.

Paragraph 5   Mrs. Tanner recognized that this diversity of languages and cultures required different teaching strategies, despite a lack of support in state funding.

Sample Summary

According to Eugene Garcia in *Student Cultural Diversity: Understanding and Meeting the Challenge,* Mrs. Tanner is a fifth-grade teacher in a typical elementary school in southern California. When she began teaching in 1981, her students had a background similar to her own, and she has emphasized active participation to promote academic achievement. However, significant changes in the student population in her school began to occur in those first ten years of her teaching career as greater numbers of African Americans and Mexicans arrived in Los Angeles to seek a better life. New arrivals of immigrants from all over the world, escaping from economic and political instability in their own countries, continued to add to the ethnic diversity of her students. **Garcia reports** that Mrs. Tanner recognized that this diversity of languages and cultures required different teaching strategies, despite a lack of support in state funding.

3. PRACTICE

Read the article "Cooperative Learning" in chapter 1. First find the main points in each paragraph. Next put these main points together to form a summary, including one or more references to the author.

Paragraph 1

_____

_____

_____

Paragraph 2

_____

_____

_____

Paragraph 3

_____

_____

_____

Summary

_____

_____

_____

_____

_____

_____

_____

_____

_____

APPENDIX V

WORD PARTS AND THEIR MEANINGS

Many longer words in English, especially academic words, contain word parts—prefixes, suffixes, and roots—that can be analyzed for meaning. Learning the meanings of these word parts can be helpful in determining the meanings of unknown words.

- A *root* has a specific meaning and can occur at the beginning, middle, or end of a word.

- A *prefix* is added at the beginning of a word.

- A *suffix* occurs at the end of a word and indicates whether the word is a noun, verb, adjective, or adverb.

English contains hundreds of word parts that entered the English language primarily from Latin and Greek. The following word parts are some of the most common and are found in many academic terms. Word parts in boldface type are presented in more detail in the chapters of this textbook, with the chapter number given in parentheses.

Roots	Meaning	Examples
agr	field	agriculture, agrarian
ann, enn	year	annual, biennial
anthrop	human	anthropology, anthropologist
aqua (16)	water	aquarium, aquatic
astro, aster	star	astrology, asteroid
audi	hear	auditorium, audience
bibli	book	bibliography, bible
bio	life	biology, biography
capit	head	capital, capitalization
card, cord	heart	cardiac, cordial
cede, ceed	go	intercede, proceed
celer	fast	accelerate, decelerate
cent	one hundred	century, percent
chron	time	chronic, chronology
clud, clus	close, shut	include, exclusion
corp	body	corpse, corporation
cosm	world	cosmos, microcosm
cred	believe	credible, credentials
dec	ten	decade, decimal
demo	people	democracy, undemocratic
dent	tooth, teeth	dentist, dental
derm	skin	dermatitis, dermatology
dict	speak	dictator, dictation
domin	master	dominate, dominion
duc, duct	lead	conductor, deduct

Roots	Meaning	Examples
fac, fic, fect	make, do	factory, fiction, defect
flect, flex	bend	reflection, flexible
frater	brother	fraternity, fraternization
gen	race, birth	gender, generation
geo	earth	geography, geology
gloss, glot	tongue	glossary, polyglot
gram, graph	write	telegram, graphic
gress, grad	step	digress, grade
hydr (16)	water	hydroelectric, dehydrate
ject	throw	reject, subject
jud	judge	judicial, judgment
lect, leg	choose, gather	collect, legion
ling, lang (14)	language	linguistics, bilingual
log	word	logic, logistics
loqu, loc	speak	loquacious, elocution
luc	light	lucid, lucidity
mania	crazy	manic, maniac
manu	hand	manual, manufacture
mar	sea	marine, submarine
mater	mother	maternity, maternal
max	more	maximum, maximize
med, mid	middle	medium, midland
mini (6)	less, little	minimum, mini
mit, miss	send	transmit, mission
mono	one	monologue, monolingual
mort	death	mortuary, mortal
multi (7)	many	multiplication, multinational
naut	sail	nautical, astronaut
neo	new	neonatal, neophyte
neuro	nerve	neuron, neurotic
nomin, nomen	name	nominate, nomenclature
pater	father	paternity, paternal
path	feelings, disease	sympathy, pathology
ped, pod	foot	pedestrian, podiatrist
pend	hang	pendant, pendulum
phil	love	philosophy, anglophile
phob	fear	phobia, claustrophobic
phon (14)	sound	telephone, phonology
phot, phos	light	photograph, phosphorus
phys	physical, body	physique, physics
plex, plic	fold	complex, complicate
poly	many	polygon, polygamous

Roots	Meaning	Examples
port (4)	carry	portable, report
pos, pon	place, put	deposit, postpone
psych (11)	mind	psychology, psychic
quad	four	quadrangle, quadruple
reg, rect	rule, right	regulation, correct
rupt	break	rupture, interrupt
scop	look	microscope, scope
scrib, script	write	scribble, description
sect	cut	dissect, section
sens, sent	feel	sensation, sentimental
soph	wise	sophisticated, philosopher
soror	sister	sorority
spec, spic	look	spectator, despicable
tact, tang	touch	tactile, tangible
tend, tens, tent	strength	tendon, tension, tentacle
terr(a)	earth	terrestrial, territory
therm	heat	thermometer, thermostat
tri	three	triple, tripod
vac	empty	vacant, vacuum
ven	come	convention, adventure
vis, vid (1)	see	vision, video
vita, viv	life	vitality, vivacious
voc, voke (19)	call	vocalize, evoke
vor	eat	herbivore, voracious

Prefixes	Meaning	Examples
ab-	away from	absent, abolish
am-	love	amicable, amorous
a-, an-	not, without	atypical, anorexia
ante-	before, in front	antebellum, anteroom
anti-	against	antiwar, antisocial
arch-	first	archbishop, architect
auto-	self	automatic, autobiography
bene-	well	benefit, benevolent
bi-	two	binary, biannual
circum-	around	circumnavigate, circumference
co-, con-, col-, cor-	with	coauthor, convention, collection, correlate
contra-, counter-	against, opposite	contrary, counteract

Prefixes	Meaning	Examples
de- dis-, di-, dif- dys-	not, away, down apart, away, not bad	deduct, descend disappear, divide, different dysfunctional, dyslexia
e-, ex- eu- extra-	out, away good outside, beyond	egress, exhale eulogy, euphoria extraordinary, extracurricular
hetero- homo- hyper- hypo-	other, different same above under	heterogeneous, heterosexual homogeneous, homosexual hyperactive, hypertension hypothetical, hypocrite
il-, ir-, im-, in- (2) inter- intra-	not among within	illegal, irrelevant, impolite, infertile interstate, interaction intrastate, intravenous
mal- mega- micro- mis-	bad, ill, wrong large, one million very small bad(ly)	malady, malfunction megacity, megabyte microscopic, microorganism mistake, misfortune
non- (2)	not	nonstop, nonsense
out- over- (17)	more more than normal	outdo, outrun oversleep, overestimate
peri- post- pre- (9) pro-	around after before forward, before	perimeter, period postpone, postdate previous, prerequisite project, promote
re- retro-	back, again backward	return, reread retroactive, retrospect
semi- sub- super-	half under over	semicircle, semicolon submarine, subway superhuman, supervise
tele- trans- (iz)	distant across	television, telephone transmit, transaction
ultra- un- (2) uni-	beyond, excessive not one	ultrasound, ultraviolet unhappy, unpleasant uniform, unique

Noun Suffixes	Meaning	Examples
-an, -ian	of, belonging to	American, Canadian
-ance, -ence	act, quality	importance, independence
-ancy, -ency	state of	vacancy, fluency
-ary, -arium	place where	library, solarium
-ary, -ess, -eer, -ant	person who	secretary, heiress, volunteer, assistant
-ation	action, institution	situation, foundation
-cide	kill	genocide, suicide
-ian, -er, -or, -ist (3)	person who	mathematician, teacher, sailor, artist
-ion, -tion, -ity	state, quality, act	union, organization, minority
-ism	quality, doctrine	communism, pessimism
-logy, -ology (8)	study	geology, astrology
-ment	act, state	statement, argument
-ness, -dom	state, quality	kindness, freedom
-ory, -orium	place where	laboratory, auditorium
-ship, -hood	state, quality	friendship, neighborhood

Adjective Suffixes	Meaning	Examples
-able, -ible (13)	able to be	capable, illegible
-al, -ative, -ent, -ic (13)	like, related to	dental, talkative, evident, atomic
-ful	having	useful, careful
-ish, -ive, -ous, -ious (13)	like, related to	stylissh, active, nervous, delicious
-less	without	useless, careless
-ly	having the quality of	womanly, friendly

Adverb Suffixes	Meaning	Examples
-ly	in the manner of	slowly, lightly
-ward	toward	forward, backward
-wise	in the manner of	clockwise, counterclockwise

Verb Suffixes	Meaning	Examples
-ate, -ify, -ize (18)	make, act	eliminate, magnify, finalize
-en (18)	make	flatten, soften

Appendix VI

THE ACADEMIC WORD LIST

This list contains the words in the form introduced in the reading texts that are included in the word families of the 570 headwords of the Academic Word List. The number after the word indicates the chapter in which the word is presented.

abandon	11	area	1	code	8	constraint	6	demonstrate	7
abstract	14	aspect	3	coherent	16	construction	3	denote	11
academic	2	assemble	18	coincide	17	consult	2	deny	19
access	7	assess	3	collapse	17	consume	4	depression	2
accommodate	12	assign	12	colleague	14	contact	12	derive	2
accompany	19	assistance	2	commence	19	contemporary	16	design	3
accumulate	17	assume	1	comment	6	context	2	despite	7
accurate	14	assure	19	commission	4	contract	3	detect	11
achieve	2	attach	18	commitment	9	contradict	19	deviation	11
acknowledge	13	attain	17	commodity	7	contrary	13	device	14
acquisition	4	attitude	9	communicate	8	contrast	8	devote	14
adaptation	14	attribute	8	community	3	contribute	7	differentiate	11
adequate	9	author	18	compensation	6	controversy	16	dimension	9
adjacent	16	authority	4	compile	19	convention	9	diminish	17
adjust	19	automatically	16	complement	16	conversely	19	discretion	13
administration	3	available	1	complex	14	convert	16	discrimination	19
adult	8	awareness	11	component	6	convey	11	displace	17
advocate	19	behalf	9	compound	9	convince	19	display	11
affect	4	benefit	1	comprehensive	16	cooperative	1	dispose	12
aggregate	18	biased	13	comprise	11	coordinate	7	distinction	4
aid	13	bond	14	computer	3	core	6	distort	11
albeit	18	brief	14	conceive	17	corporation	7	distribution	3
allocate	13	bulk	18	concentrate	8	correspondingly	6	diversity	6
alter	6	capable	11	concept	1	couple	16	document	7
alternative	13	capacity	11	conclusion	14	create	2	domain	13
ambiguous	14	category	4	concurrent	19	credit	4	domestic	7
amend	19	cease	19	conducive	2	criteria	19	dominant	6
analogous	11	challenge	9	confer	18	crucial	16	draft	19
analysis	1	channel	13	confine	16	cultural	4	dramatic	17
annual	7	chapter	4	confirm	17	currency	9	duration	17
anticipate	16	chart	19	conflict	11	cycle	8	dynamic	12
apparent	8	chemical	9	conform	17	data	1	economic	1
append	4	circumstance	6	consent	19	debate	14	edit	1
appreciate	19	cite	14	consequence	4	decade	6	element	3
approach	1	civilian	19	considerable	6	decline	9	eliminate	16
appropriate	2	clarify	17	consistent	2	deduce	11	emergence	8
approximate	7	classic	2	constant	6	define	2	emigration	12
arbitrary	19	clause	14	constitute	4	definite	11	emphasis	6

empirical	17	formula	1	infinite	18	likewise	11	option	9
enable	12	forthcoming	16	infrastructure	13	link	7	orientation	3
encounter	18	found	17	inherently	14	location	6	outcome	6
energy	4	foundation	18	inhibit	17	logical	17	output	8
enforce	12	framework	6	initial	6	maintenance	3	overall	8
enhancement	12	function	2	initiative	16	major	1	overlap	17
enormous	17	fundamental	11	injure	4	manipulate	14	overseas	13
ensure	6	funds	6	innovative	7	manual	12	panel	16
entity	9	furthermore	11	input	12	marginal	11	paradigm	16
environment	2	gender	19	insertion	18	maturity	14	paragraph	18
equation	4	generate	9	insight	19	maximize	7	parallel	2
equipment	13	generation	11	inspect	18	mechanism	9	parameter	9
equivalent	11	global	8	instability	12	media	8	participate	4
erosion	16	goal	8	instance	8	mediate	19	partnership	7
error	2	grade	6	institutional	3	medical	12	passive	16
establish	1	grant	9	instruction	14	mental	11	perceive	3
estate	12	guarantee	18	integral	16	method	1	percent	2
estimate	2	guideline	18	integration	6	military	7	period	1
ethical	8	hence	8	integrity	19	minimal	14	persistent	16
ethnic	6	hierarchy	12	intelligence	14	minimize	16	perspective	12
evaluate	3	highlight	18	intense	18	minimum	16	phase out	7
eventually	16	hypothesize	9	interaction	6	ministry	16	phenomenon	17
evidence	1	identical	11	intermediate	6	minority	6	philosophy	6
evolve	11	identify	1	internal	8	mode	19	physical	8
exceed	12	ideological	12	interpretation	1	modifiable	11	plus	8
exclude	8	ignore	13	interval	13	monitor	9	policy	3
exhibit	11	illustrate	6	interventionist	13	motivation	12	portion	18
expansion	12	image	9	intrinsically	11	mutual	14	pose	11
expert	14	immigrant	6	investment	4	negative	7	positive	3
explicit	19	impact	2	investigation	9	network	12	potential	2
exploitation	12	implement	7	invoke	17	neutral	13	practitioner	18
export	4	implicate	18	involve	1	nevertheless	14	precede	17
exposure	12	implicitly	12	isolated	14	nonetheless	16	precisely	9
external	18	imply	8	issue	1	norm	11	predict	9
extract	13	impose	7	item	2	normally	4	predominant	16
facilitate	11	incentive	12	job	6	notion	11	preliminary	14
factor	1	incidence	12	journalist	4	notwithstand-		presumption	13
feature	18	incline	16	justification	7	ing	14	previously	4
federal	16	income	2	label	8	nuclear	16	primarily	13
fee	13	incompatible	14	labor	3	objective	8	primary	3
file	19	incorporate	14	layer	17	obtain	3	principal	8
final	3	index	19	lecture	4	obvious	9	principle	4
financial	2	indicate	1	legal	2	occupational	9	prior	9
flexible	11	individual	1	legislation	4	occur	1	priority	13
fluctuation	16	induce	18	levy	6	odd	18	proceed	18
focus	4	inevitably	16	liberal	13	offset	16	process	1
format	14	infer	14	license	2	ongoing	14	professional	7

prohibit	19	reliance	6	sequence	16	sum	19	transportation	12
project	8	reluctance	19	series	7	summary	14	trend	13
promotion	7	removal	8	sex	6	supplement	16	trigger	17
proportion	6	require	2	shift	6	survey	3	ultimately	12
prospect	18	research	1	significant	1	survival	12	undergo	7
protocol	13	reside	3	similar	1	suspend	18	underlying	12
psychologist	2	resolve	7	simulate	11	sustain	12	undertake	7
publication	13	resource	4	site	3	symbolic	9	uniform	16
publish	7	respond	2	so-called	17	tape	13	unify	14
purchase	3	restoration	19	sole	17	target	8	unique	14
pursuit	12	restrain	16	somewhat	13	task	6	utility	3
qualitative	11	restrict	3	source	2	team	1	valid	9
quote	18	retain	9	specific	1	technical	19	variables	1
radical	12	reveal	11	specify	8	technique	6	vehicle	16
random	4	revenue	9	sphere	19	technology	8	version	17
range	2	reverse	17	statistics	8	temporarily	9	via	13
ratio	13	revise	17	status	8	tense	2	violate	14
rationalization	13	revolution	12	straightfor-ward	19	terminate	18	virtual	13
react	6	rigid	19			text	2	visible	12
recovery	18	role	1	strategy	3	theme	19	vision	6
refine	4	route	19	stress	2	theoretical	1	visual	18
regime	9	scenario	16	structure	1	thereby	16	volume	7
region	4	schedule	4	style	11	thesis	1	voluntary	4
register	7	scheme	7	submit	18	topic	19	welfare	2
regulation	3	scope	13	subordinate	12	trace	16	whereas	9
reinforce	19	section	2	subsequent	7	traditionally	4	whereby	17
reject	18	sector	2	subsidy	16	transfer (transfor-mation) 3 (12)		widespread	17
relax	2	security	3	substitute	13				
release	16	seek	2	successive	16	transition	12		
relevant	4	select	3	sufficient	6	transmission	13		